S0-AXX-258

Death Note
Fatally Fun Facts

cocoro books

Published by DH Publishing, Inc.
1-20-2-518 Higashiikebukuro, Toshima-Ku
Tokyo 170-0013, Japan

http://www.dhp-online.com

cocoro books is an imprint of DH Publishing, Inc.
First Published 2008

Text and illustrations ©2008 by DH Publishing, Inc.
Printed in CHINA
Printed by Miyuki Inter-Media Hong Kong, Inc.

ISBN 978-1-932897-32-6

By courtesy of Akio Kurono (cac co,ltd.)

Summary

When a god of death, or shinigami, named Ryuk gets bored and drops into the human world a Death Note, a notebook that kills any humans whose names are written in it, Light Yagami happens to pick it up. Soon he is wiping out criminals one after another in the hope of creating an ideal world. The legendary detective L considers this mass murder and goes after him. Thus begins the story of Death Note.

The first print of the first manga volume sold one million copies and set a manga sales record. In 2004, the same year it was released, it made it onto Japan's 10 bestsellers list for the year. Together, all 12 volumes of the story have sold over 25.3 million copies; an average of more than two million per volume.

By revealing the criminal and his crimes first and then how the detective tries to track him down, Death Note is clearly in the genre of the "inverted detective story." Another element is the circular plot, in which Light tries to catch L, Mello, and Near, while at the same time they try to catch him. The story is fast-paced, it has strong rhythm, and it steers clear of compromising itself with preachy messages. The story is structured around good and evil, but it leaves it to the reader to come to his or her own conclusions.

The serialization of Death Note continued, and eventually it developed a first and second part. The first part features L as the main detective, and the second features Near.

Plot Overview

First Part

One day, Light Yagami, a high school student, finds an unusual black notebook. It is a Death Note. It was dropped by Ryuk, a shinigami, or god of death. Whoever's name is written in it dies.

Light begins to use it to kill the world's criminals. His goal is to end crime and build a brave new world. The public soon becomes aware that someone is responsible for the deaths and name him "Kira," from the English "Killer" (it also can mean "sparkle" in Japanese and is a marginally common name). Some people even begin to worship Kira as a god.

Meanwhile, the ICPO (Interpol), has learnt about this Kira character and calls on the mystery detective L, known for being able to crack any case and the only one to have the respect of the world's police forces. L, who treats Kira as evil, uses unusual but logically sound methods to establish that Kira is in the Kanto region of Japan, sets up his central investigation headquarters there, and challenges Kira. Kira and L each have their own version of justice. The battle begins.

Second Part

It is 2009 and five years have passed since the death of L. Light has inherited his name and position as the secret leader of the police. At the same time, he continues his alter ego existence of Kira, executing criminals for the purpose of creating an ideal society. He has the support of the masses. Even governments are falling. in line.

Meanwhile, the orphanage that raised L, Wammy's House, produces two "successors," Near and Mello. Near becomes the head of a new U.S. agency, the Secret Provision for Kira (SPK), and a threat to Light. Mello takes control of a crime organization, kidnaps Light's little sister Sayu, and demands to be given the Death Note at the Japanese Kira investigation headquarters.

Light continues as Kira while acting the part of L, still committed to his vision of justice and the perfect world. But his nemeses, Near and Mello, are closing in.

CONTENTS

Chapter 01

The Shinigami's Secrets

I n the world of Death Note, besides the human world, Heaven and Hell, there is also a shinigami world where shinigami (gods of death) like Ryuk and Rem live.

When Ryuk first appears before Light, he casts considerable doubt upon whether the shinigami really have much purpose at all, saying, "I dropped the Death Note in the human world because I was bored" and "It sounds weird for a shinigami to be saying this, but I don't feel like I'm alive. Nowadays, practically all we do is hang around, nap, and gamble." Furthermore, he says, "Shinigami these days never say, 'I don't like this human,' or, 'Let's make the human world better,' or, 'Lets make the human world worse.' We couldn't really care less." "We just live on vaguely because we vaguely feel we don't want to die, and so we take people's lives." "The shinigami world has really decayed." "No one knows anymore why we even exist." It seems as if shinigami aren't even necessary.

However, it also implies that shinigami originally did have a purpose for the human world, and that, once, the shinigami did say "I don't like this human" and "Let's make the human world better."

Long ago, people believed that gods of death (shinigami)

caused people to die by taking their souls out of their bodies. But, apparently, people have a set life span in the first place after which they will die even if shinigami don't do anything. The shinigami know that they can be as lazy as they want to and people will still die. However, the shinigami can live on by partaking of the remaining life spans of humans. A shinigami who wants to be sure to live longer could make an effort to take more human lives, except that humans would then become extinct, and consequently, with their life supply gone, so would the shinigami. So the shinigami must take life cautiously. Also, a human likely to kill many other humans would be a more logical target, so as to keep the human race alive and plentiful for the shinigami. Thus, one would expect shinigami to serve the purpose of helping to perpetuate the human race.

Present-day shinigami, however, like Ryuk, don't get involved with the human world. This explains the human population explosion and its corresponding strain on Earth's environment and natural resources. The current laziness of shinigami may spell doom for the human race, as well as for the shinigami themselves.

In short: the probable purpose of the gods of death is to keep people alive.

02 What is the shinigami world like?

Apparently, it's boring, just as shinigami Ryuk complains. There is no pressing work to keep shinigami busy—all they have to do is take some lives once in a while and they can live on forever in their humdrum world. The shinigami world doesn't seem to be blessed with physical resources, either. The shinigami gamble to entertain themselves, but they don't appear to have any better tools than human skulls. There are apples, like the one Ryuk brings to the human world, but they are "sandy," dry and unappetizing, which Ryuk makes clear with his voracious love of the apples of the human world. However, there is a rule that shinigami can't hang around in the human world without a special reason to be there, such as if they dropped their Death Note, so, normally, even though the world of the humans seems richer, the shinigami can only look and point at it.

Death Note does not give a full picture of all aspects of the shinigami world. For instance, it's unclear how big it is or how many shinigami there are. However, it does seem to be above the human world, somehow, so that the shinigami can look "down." There are no signs of family structures in the shinigami world, but there is a "shinigami king" (although he never appears); it seems there must be some sort of organized social structure with different classes.

In any case, it doesn't seem like a very appealing place to live, although the shinigami are "gods." They must have had this stoic life thrust upon them.

03 What is the purpose of the Death Note?

Shinigami are obliged to own at least one Death Note. They need it to take the lives of humans whose names they write in it to add to their own life spans; a shinigami without a Death Note will eventually die.

But the shinigami in the human world are able to physically interact with it–they move objects around, eat apples, etc. They should be able to easily wring a human's neck without any need for a Death Note. They're basically invincible. They can't be harmed by weapons. They can slip through walls and fly through the air. Why, then, do they need a complicated system that requires them to write the name of the person they wish to kill in a notebook? There is even harsh punishment for using any other method. Why?

When humans such as Light get their hands on the Death Note, they can use it in the same way a shinigami can. Or one could say that the Death Note is made so that humans can use it. Perhaps it was even made to be dropped into the human world. There are detailed rules for this situation. One rule, for instance, is that there may be up to six Death Notes in the human world. If there is a seventh, even if a human uses it, it won't work. The very existence of this rule proves that having seven Death Notes in the human world is seen as a possibility.

There are many other minor rules about what happens when multiple Death Notes are used in the human world. There would be no point in making so many rules unless, as is probably the case, there is a need for them. Moreover, Death Notes involve the cultures of the human world. For instance, Light has to write names with their kanji for the effect to work. The Death Note definitely seems to have been designed for humans.

In general, each shinigami has one Death Note. This would mean that the number of shinigami equals the number of Death Notes. Therefore, the most likely situation for a Death Note to end up in the human world is if the number of shinigami drops, allowing for surplus Death Notes. Two shinigami die over the course of the story, Jealous and Rem (Jealous even without Light's intervention). It's clear that the number of shinigami must occasionally drop. If this goes on without creating any new shinigami, the number will eventually become zero. In the beginning, Ryuk tells Light that using the Death Note won't allow him to go to Heaven or condemn him to Hell. Near the end, it is stated that humans are reduced to nothing when they die, but perhaps Light will actually go to the shinigami world and become a shinigami. Perhaps the Death Note is the mechanism for creating new shinigami. That would explain why it seems to be designed for humans.

04 How long have the Death Notes existed?

Death Notes, in their current form, could not have worked before humans invented writing. This suggests that they did not exist until, at the earliest, some 6,000 years ago. But humans have been around much longer. Shinigami probably have been, too. It is unknown how old the shinigami of the story are. However, because shinigami can live indefinitely, it would not be surprising if some of them were over 6,000 years old.

It is stated that shinigami are unable to procreate with humans or each other. Yet there are male and female shinigami. Rem points out her gender very casually to Misa, and so it seems this concept is one the shinigami very much take for granted. Perhaps the different shinigami sexes are a remnant of a previous time when they were human. There must have been some sort of system predating the written word that allowed humans to become shinigami, one that didn't involve writing in a notebook.

It follows that there has been a covenant between humans and shinigami since long, long ago, but it's only relatively recently that it has taken on the form of a notebook.

05 Do shinigami have to haunt the person who uses their Death Note?

I n the rules for humans using the Death Note, there are many clauses binding the shinigami. Among them are, "The person in possession of the DEATH NOTE is possessed by a god of death, its original owner, until they die," and "If a human uses the note, a god of death usually appears in front of him/her within 39 days after he/she uses the note." This implies that the shinigami generally have to show up in 39 days and have a duty to keep watch over the human. The conditions under which they can leave are:

1. When the god of death has seen the end of the first owner of the DEATH NOTE brought into the human world, and has written that human's name on his/her own DEATH NOTE.

2. When the DEATH NOTE which has been brought in is destroyed, like burned, and cannot be used by humans anymore.

3. If nobody claims the ownership of the DEATH NOTE and it is unnecessary to haunt anyone.

4. If, for any reason, the god of death possessing the DEATH

NOTE has been replaced by another god of death.

5. When the god of death loses track of the DEATH NOTE which he/she possesses, cannot identify which human is owning the DEATH NOTE, or cannot locate where the owner is, and therefore needs to find such information through the hole in the world of gods of death.

Even in situations 2, 3, and 4 above, gods of death are obliged to confirm the death of the first owner and write down that person's name in his/her Death Note, even when he/she is in the world of gods of death.

In short, once a human claims a shinigami's Death Note, the shinigami is only allowed to return home when the human dies or the Death Note is destroyed, or if another shinigami takes over surveillance of the person in question. Also, shinigami are free to answer questions by humans about how to use the Death Note as they please. However, it seems it's not acceptable for them to give advice such as "Kill this guy" or "Don't kill that guy." Almost all explanations center on the methods of killing and death, but there aren't any rules like, "You can't use it for self-defense"; in short, humans have more or less complete freedom over what to do with the Death Note. For the shinigami, on the other hand, having a human use their Death Note places additional limitations and duties on them. There doesn't seem to be much advantage. The last sentence even uses the word "obliged," a good summary of the shinigami's overall situation here. "Gods of death are obliged to confirm the death of the first owner and write down that human's name." This sounds as if the shinigami and humans have a contract. This makes it all the more logical for the shinigami to have an obligation to watch over humans.

Perhaps the harshest limitation placed on shinigami is that "If the god of death decides to use the DEATH NOTE to kill the assassin of an individual he favors, the individual's life will be extended, but the god of death will die." This doesn't apply to humans, who are quite free to kill anyone they want. Shinigami have to kill to live and have so many restrictions about how to do so. The Death Note is an extremely convenient murder weapon for a human, but not at all for a shinigami.

06 Who created the Death Notes?

Each shinigami is obliged to own one Death Note, without which, they cannot extend their lives. Since there seems to be almost no regulations for humans using the Death Note (at least until they die, when they may be obliged to become shinigami), but shinigami have to follow numerous and complicated rules, it is likely that the Death Notes were created by the "great god of death" (or "great shinigami king"). The great god of death might be the original shinigami and the only one who wasn't originally a human. He may exist to regulate the human world by means of death. It may be the case that he himself never dies—he is absolute, eternal, the true god. Perhaps he created the shinigami world and then created the Death Notes to be able to manage the deaths of more humans. The humans who use the Death Note, then, are entering into a contract to become shinigami. They then have to kill to stay alive.

Every so often, when shinigami die, their Death Notes are left in the human world. The human who has the power to wield the Death Note in the human world, in other words, the human who can kill humans, is logically the most fit to manage death as a shinigami. The rules of the Death Note say that "If a human uses the note, a god of death usually appears in front of him/her within 39 days after he/she uses the note." This is only "If a human uses the note," not if a human merely picks up the note and looks at it. Using it means killing. So, only humans who can kill humans become shinigami.

By this logic, the Death Note seems very carefully planned as an effective scouting device for shinigami to manage death. It is all the more logical, then, for the great god of death to have been the one who created it.

07 Are shinigami prohibited from meddling in human affairs?

The only time shinigami are allowed to hang around in the human world is when a human uses their Death Note, in which case the shinigami must watch over the human. Otherwise, their only allowed purpose in the human world is to look for people to kill. Even when they are allowed to be in the human world, they aren't allowed to otherwise interfere with it. This is evident from the way Ryuk treats apples. No one can see him, except for the few who have touched his Death Note, and it would be easy for him to snatch a few of his favorite fruit. Instead, he has Light buy them for him. There must be some rules regulating shinigami's interactions in the human world.

Another shinigami, Sidoh, on the other hand, takes it upon himself to help Mello by actually snatching off the helmets the police are wearing to protect themselves from the Death Note. When they come to take back the Death Note from Mello, Snydar intervenes and Mello is able to kill them. This certainly seems to be interfering in the human world. However, in this case, Mello's Death Note was Sidoh's to begin with, and, since Sidoh isn't very smart, he figures he'll need Mello's cooperation to get it back. So perhaps Sidoh's interference was simply allowed as an inadvertent necessity.

When Misa is shackled by L under suspicion of being the "second Kira," Rem, who likes Misa, offers to undo her restraints and let her escape. In the end, this doesn't happen, but only because Misa is against the plan. This would have also been distinct interference in the human world. It seems that this kind of action is not prohibited, but strongly discouraged, although it is left to the shinigami to make the final decision. Perhaps the fact that Ryuk does not take apples by himself is just his own personal policy. And, even though Ryuk tends to keep his hands to himself, he does interfere at a physical distance by helping Light search his room for hidden cameras and alerting him to the FBI agent, Raye Penber, trailing him.

According to one of the manga's "HOW TO USE IT" pages:

"There are laws in the world of gods of death. If a god of death should break the law, there are 9 levels of severity starting at Level 8 and going up to Level 1 plus the Extreme Level. For severity levels above 3 the god of death will be killed after being punished.

"For example, killing a human without using the DEATH NOTE is considered as the Extreme Level."

08 Are shinigami allowed to lie to humans?

Shinigami are remarkably lacking in freedom, bound tightly by their duty to manage human death. It isn't even seen as acceptable for shinigami to sleep; since it's not necessary for them, it's regarded as laziness.

However, there doesn't seem to be any rule against shinigami lying to humans. Ryuk, cooperating with Light, writes false rules in a Death Note and tricks the police. Ryuk also suggests that shinigami do not necessarily have to answer questions humans ask them about how to use the Death Note. The shinigami even claim that the false rules are true when asked. Shinigami may be governed by strict laws, but they are not necessarily consistent with what humans consider "good," and shinigami are not prohibited from doing "wrong," such as lying.

09 Do humans with shinigami eyes see what shinigami do?

All shinigami have "shinigami eyes," with abilities foreign to humans. For example, by viewing part of a person's face, they can tell the person's name and life span. The Death Note can only kill someone when the user writes that person's name down with their face in mind. Therefore, in most cases, even if the target's face is known, the Death Note will not work without knowledge of that person's name. However, because shinigami always see a person's name with that person's face, effectively, seeing the human's face is all that is required.

Humans can attain this power, too, by trading in half their remaining life span to a shinigami. Misa does this twice. Higuchi, Snydar, Light's father, and Mikami also do it.

Although touching a shinigami's Death Note allows a person to see and speak to the shinigami regardless of whether he or she owns the Death Note, the person must own the Death Note to attain "shinigami eyes." Also, as soon as one surrenders one's ownership of the Death Note, one loses the power.

Even with the power, "a person with the DEATH NOTE cannot see the life span of other DEATH NOTE owners, including him/herself," under the logic that "By possessing the

DEATH NOTE, an individual gains the ability to kill and stops being a victim" and "it is not really necessary for the individual to view the life span of him/herself nor other DEATH NOTE owners." Misa exploits this to identify Kira as Light, looking out into the street and finding the only one whose life span she couldn't see (and seeing his name).

However, humans with shinigami eyes do not see the same as shinigami. Even though Misa possesses a Death Note, Rem sees when her life span is cut in half for the second time.

I t would not be unreasonable to ask whether someone with a Death Note can shorten the life span that they see. However, the answer would be an emphatic "No."

What one sees is a person's "original" life span, which does not take into account being killed by a Death Note. Anyone killed with a Death Note was originally going to live longer. The length of life taken from a shinigami victim is added to the shinigami's own life. Even if one is fated to be killed with a Death Note, that fate is not visible. If it were, it would be impossible for shinigami to continue to live, because there would never be any difference between the originally expected time of death and the time the human dies at the hands of a shinigami.

There is a point at which Light's life span is visible through Ryuk's eyes. At that point, Light has already acquired the Death Note, so the life span Ryuk sees might actually reflect the effects of the Death Note—it can't directly reflect Ryuk's killing Light, but the actions Light takes because of the Death Note would have likely shortened his life anyway.

If someone killed him, by human methods, to get the Death Note, that would already be accounted for in his "original" life span shown in shinigami eyes (as is made clear by the shinigami rule against killing a human to save another, which, it is said, would lengthen their life spans). Being killed with a Death Note is the only way to die that is not accounted for in advance in the "original" life span. It's hard to say if Light's receiving a Death Note shortens his original life span at that point, but, whether then or before, it certainly affects his original life span. There is always only one number, and not multiple ones for different conditions of getting or not getting a Death Note.

However, when humans receive shinigami eyes, their original life spans are changed. Rem is able to see from Misa's life span that she has made the bargain for the second time, cutting her remaining life in half. This is a situation in which a human Death Note user makes a conscious decision regarding his or her own longevity. (One could make the argument that suicide has a similar effect.)

In general, shinigami see a fixed life span for each human that lets them know exactly when that human is going to die, as long as the human isn't killed with a Death Note.

One last exception occurs when shinigami break the rules. When the shinigami Jealous and Rem save Misa, that adds to her life span. This is an unusual situation in which shinigami die and give their lives to humans.

11 · *How do shinigami die?*

Shinigami are basically immortal, since they can indefinitely kill people and add their life spans to their own, but they do have a limited life span if they fail to kill.

They also die if they intentionally use their Death Notes to save a particular human, which is against the rules. This is perhaps the strictest shinigami rule. There are many other rules, like those against them entering the human world without a specific reason and against letting people know of the presence of other shinigami. However, this rule is the only one that if broken results in a shinigami's permanent disappearance. It is therefore considered one of the most important rules. (It is mentioned, however, that some violations result in a more painful death than that of Rem.)

The shinigami Jealous is aware that fate dictates that Misa be stabbed and killed by a stalker. However, he uses a Death Note to kill the stalker before he gets to Misa. In this case, it's obvious that he used the Death Note, and therefore he must die. In Rem's case, however, L suspects Misa, and it is likely that if he caught her, she would be given the death penalty. However, this isn't a foregone conclusion. However, Rem disappears after killing L and Watari. The rule is that a god of death may not use the Death Note "to kill the assassin of an individual he favors," and it seems the "to" does not merely mean "with the effect of killing the assassin," but even "for the purpose of killing the assassin" even if the actual effect is unknown. It's very strict.

Ryuk mentions to Light that, even though one can't kill a shinigami by writing his or her name in the Death Note, there are other ways of killing shinigami. However, these methods are never explained in the story.

12 Are shinigami allowed to help humans with Death Notes?

pparently, shinigami aren't supposed to help or hinder a person who uses a Death Note, but it seems to be a lax rule that is not particularly enforced and occasionally bent.

However, shinigami are not allowed to reveal to the person with the Death Note the names or life spans of others humans. It seems to be part of the shinigami moral code not to interfere too recklessly with the human world.

Sidoh interferes when the police attack the mafia headquarters. His purpose however is not to help humans, but to retrieve his Death Note. He doesn't have much choice in the matter, which is probably why his actions are treated lightly.

In contrast, shinigami are free to kill humans holding Death Notes. After all, a shinigami's existence depends solely on killing humans, whenever and wherever. However, a human in possession of a Death Note can only be killed by the shinigami that gave him or her the Death Note in the first place. That human is off-limits to all other shinigami.

Shinigami clearly have no obligation to explain the rules to any human using a Death Note, although the rules themselves aren't secret. The shinigami apparently tell humans whatever they feel like telling them.

Tsugumi Ohba: The Mystery of the Author

Death Note is a collaboration between writer Tsugumi Ohba and artist Takeshi Obata. Obata was famous before Death Note, especially for the hit Hikaru no Go, but this was Ohba's first credit.

To get into Shukan Shonen Jump (Weekly Boys' Jump), the most popular manga magazine in Japan, an artist/author is expected to have at least a few competition wins under his or her belt. Ohba debuted without any previous writing credits.

Yet, he had Death Note so tightly structured that he quickly became a major topic of discussion on the Internet. Was "Ohba" the penname of a veteran author? The first to come under suspicion was the author known simply as Otsuichi.

Otsuichi launched his novel-writing career in 1996 after winning the 6th Jump Novels and Nonfiction Awards Grand Prize with "Summer, Fireworks, and My Dead Body" at the tender age of 17 (he had written it a year before). He was linked to Shonen Jump and was known for his mystery-writing skills. The possible link with "Ohba" was discussed widely.

From then on, various authors surfaced in online discussions as possible alter ego candidates for Tsugumi Ohba, but evidence remained circumstantial.

In interviews, Ohba described himself as a new author. Shueisha has never made any official comment.

In May 2006, on the ABC Radio program Makoto no Psychic Seinendan (Makoto's Psychic Youth Force), of which Shueisha is a sponsor, the author Yoshikazu Takeuchi, speaking about the Death Note movie adaptation, stated that Ohba is "actually a major author who's been around the block a few times" and that Ohba's identity is "top secret even among the Jump editorial staff. Even among the people who are closely connected to him, not many know who he is."

The author now considered most likely to be Ohba is Hiroshi Gamo. Gamo has had his work, such as Tottemo! Lucky Man (Very! Lucky Man), serialized in Shonen Jump. And stronger evidence exists. Consider these three facts::

1. The cram school Light attends at the very beginning of Death Note is called "Gamo Seminar."

2. Each edition of Shonen Jump is arranged with the stories voted most popular by readers at the front. Therefore, some people involved call the last pages of the magazine the "Batsu-Gumi" (X-Mark Group). Therefore, "Ohba Tsugumi" (the Japanese ordering of "Tsugumi Ohba") may be a self-deprecating pen name based on the author's previous experience in Shonen Jump: "Oh-Batsu-Gumi." (Some also say that Oh-Batsu-Gumi was the name of a fan-comic team Gamo was in.)

3. Hiroshi Gamo has had experience writing mystery manga, such as Boku wa Shonen Tantei Dan (I'm Boy Detective Dan).

Chapter 02

The Death Note Secrets

13 How do humans benefit from using a Death Note?

The Death Note is fundamentally a tool that allows shinigami to acquire the remaining life spans of humans. To do this, a shinigami must write the target victim's name in the notebook. For instance, if a shinigami writes the name of a 25-year-old who was originally going to die at 70, the human dies forty-five years ahead of his time and the shinigami gains forty-five years.

However, this same doesn't happen when humans use Death Notes. The remaining life spans of their victims are not added to their own lives. The advantage a human gains from using a Death Note is that he or she can murder someone without leaving incriminating evidence. Humans also have the advantage of using a Death Note to kill with impunity to save others. Shinigami that do the same are reduced to ash. For humans, it seems like the ideal weapon.

When Light first uses the Death Note, he probably expects some sort of retribution. When Ryuk shows up, he probably believes the time has come for him to pay for the killing. However, this is not the case. Can killing really be free?

Ryuk says that humans who use the Death Note can go to neither Heaven nor Hell. Light responds with, "That just means Heaven and Hell don't exist, doesn't it?"

"Death is the same no matter what good or evil things humans do when they're alive. Death is equal."

Near the end, the author Tsugumi Ohba writes, "When they [humans] die, the place they go is MU (Nothingness)."

It's clear that this is true from the point of view of the living. Regardless of who they are, when they die, they no longer exist to those who are still alive. What it is like from the point of view of the dead, however, remains unclear. When Ryuk points out that those who use the Death Note can't go to Heaven or Hell, there must be a reason for him to say this. There are consequences of using Death Notes after all. As explained in the first chapter, there is strong evidence that Death Notes are actually mechanisms to turn humans into shinigami. The reason Light can't go to Heaven or Hell is that he will be going to the shinigami world. This has much greater repercussions than merely being locked up in prison for life or dying earlier than expected.

14 Is it possible to escape from deaths written in the Death Note?

I f someone writes a person's name in a Death Note while picturing their face, but doesn't write anything else, that person will die of a heart attack in 40 seconds. It is possible to specify the method and circumstances of death, such as, "Dies in an accident when X happens" or "Dies of a heart attack after doing Y," or to specify the time of death. However, once the name is written, the death becomes unstoppable.

If impossible circumstances are given for a person's death, such as, "Randomly gets hit by a meteor and dies" or "Dies two hours from now on the other side of the world," that person will still die, but of a heart attack in 40 seconds, just as if no circumstances had been written. Even if the person who wrote the name changes his or her mind, whether by erasing or scratching out what has been written, it is too late to save the target victim.

However, there are situations in which writing someone's name won't have the desired effect. First is if the writer doesn't know what the person looks like. This is to safeguard against people with the same name being accidentally killed. Otherwise, if one wrote, for example, "John Smith," everyone in the world named John Smith would die. That's why the writer needs to imagine in their mind's eye the face of the specific person he or she wants dead. If one doesn't know what the person looks like, then the Death Note doesn't work.

Even if one does know what the prospective victim looks like, if that person's real, full and correct name is not written, nothing will happen. L shows his face to Light, but he always uses pseudonyms such as "L," "Lyuga," or "Lyuzaki." This allows him to escape from the effects of the Death Note.

However, if the Death Note user acquires shinigami eyes, he or she can find out a target victim's name simply by looking at his or her face.

Another rule that can save a potential victim is the one that stipulates, "If a DEATH NOTE owner accidentally misspells a name four times, that person will be free from being killed by the DEATH NOTE." Therefore, if Light had tried to kill L by writing the names "L," "Lyuzaki," and "Hideki Lyuga," then he would have had only one more chance to write L's correct name before it became impossible for him ever to kill L with the Death Note. From the Japanese wording, it appears that "the DEATH NOTE" from which a person is freed by such circumstances refers to all Death Notes, not just the one in which the name is written incorrectly, and that this is the case regardless of who is doing the writing.

This raises the question of whether Light could have Misa write his name incorrectly on purpose four times so that no one could ever kill him with a Death Note. "However," the rules also say, "if they intentionally misspell the name four times, the DEATH NOTE owner will die," and "The person whose name was misspelled four times on purpose will not be free of death by a DEATH NOTE." So, this strategy would only work if Misa was honestly trying to kill him, didn't know his real name, and thought the names she was writing might be his real names.

Finally, the simplest way to escape the Death Note is to be over 124 years old, because "You cannot kill humans at the age of 124 and over with the DEATH NOTE." So, if Light managed to live to such an age, he would be safe, at least from Ryuk.

15 How flexible is the rule regarding names written in a Death Note?

Only a human's legal name works. If one knows what a popular author looks like and the pen name by which that author is famous, one still won't be able to kill him or her unless their legal name is written.

In the case of Japanese names, there is the question of whether they must be written in kanji. Even if "Tato Yamada" is written in kanji, hiragana, katakana, or Roman letters, it would still generally be considered the same name and not misspelled, although the kanji version is the official one. It is clear that Light assumes that he must write Japanese names in kanji. He writes his second victim's name, Takuo Shibuimaru, in seven different possible combinations of kanji that would have the correct pronunciation to try to get the right name. It turns out that, by chance, Light got it right the first time, which is why Shibuimaru was, in fact, killed in an accident. If Light hadn't got it right till the fifth try or after, Shibuimaru would be forevermore invincible to all Death Notes, because Light would have already misspelled his name four times. Obviously, Light didn't fully understand how to use the Death Note. It is possible that he could have just written "Shibuimaru Takuo" in phonetic katakana and it would have worked. However, Light continues to always write Japanese names in kanji, despite his many experiments in how to use the Death Note, many of which are not shown, but only mentioned afterwards. Therefore, it is likely that Light does, in fact, conclude by experiment that Japanese names have to be written the official kanji way.

16 What's this about Death Note "ownership"?

It makes a big difference who owns a Death Note. A Death Note originally comes from a shinigami, who oversees it even while it is in a particular human's hands. The human user is allowed to lend it out freely, and anyone can write in it to kill someone. The shinigami has to stay with the person who has the Death Note. It makes a difference whether the human gives the Death Note away or merely lends it out. If the human lends it out, the shinigami stays put, presumably because the notebook is expected to be returned. If a human gives it away, the shinigami leaves the original owner to follow the new owner.

Ownership of the Death Note, then, rests heavily on the mere intentions of humans. When a Death Note is first dropped into the human world, no one owns it; when someone picks it up, that person becomes the first human owner, regardless of intentions. If the person then gets rid of the Death Note with the thought that they don't want it anymore, that absolves their ownership. But this will erase all their memories related to it. They will no longer even remember that there are such things as Death Notes and shinigami. This will also cancel the effects of shinigami eyes if they have them, without bringing back the half of their life span they gave up for the eyes. The exception to these rules is that, if, despite owning the Death Note, they never used it, they won't lose their memories of it.

Regardless of whether a human owns a particular Death Note, however, touching it allows the human to see the shinigami that watches over that Death Note. On the other hand, if one gains ownership of the Death Note and then surrenders ownership, one loses the ability to see the shinigami, despite still being able to remember that it and the Death Note exist.

Even if one owns a Death Note, one can't see the shinigami that watch over other Death Notes, unless one touches those Death Notes.

17 Can one keep the Death Note's ownership indefinitely?

One can give up the Death Note's ownership just by mentally deciding that one doesn't want it anymore, but there are also ways to lose ownership unintentionally. First, it can be stolen. When the Death Note is first stolen, one retains ownership, but, if one doesn't retrieve the notebook within 490 days, one will lose ownership. The same goes for misplacing the notebook. When one loses ownership, one also loses all one's memories regarding the Death Note, making it even more unlikely that one will ever get it back (since one won't even remember that it exists in the first place, and, even if one finds out about it again, one is unlikely to have the same motivation to get it, or knowledge, for that matter).

If one dies, one loses ownership. This could make a thief kill the owner to get ownership in less than 490 days, which would work immediately if the thief had physical possession of the Death Note.

In the rare situation that someone owns two Death Notes, that person can give up the ownership of one Death Note and still keep the memories associated with both.

Even if one loses ownership of the Death Note and therefore one's memories of it, if one can get back the ownership, one's memories come back. If one hasn't regained ownership, one can still temporarily regain one's memories just by touching the notebook, until one lets go. This can occur up to six times for each Death Note. One touches the notebook, and one's memories come back; one lets go, and the memories go away again; starting the seventh time, the memories don't come back anymore, and it's as if the holder is just touching the Death Note for the first time.

The loss of memory associated with losing the Death Note is probably why humans don't know about the Death Note as of the beginning of the story, even though Death Notes have circulated in the human world before. Ryuk gives Light a Death Note to use as he pleases in order to relieve Ryuk's boredom, but otherwise there is no particular advantage to the shinigami in humans knowing about the Death Note. So, even if a shinigami drops a Death Note in the human world by accident and a human picks it up, if the human gives it up, it appears as if it didn't happen. The Death Note was probably made this way in order to cover such mistakes.

18 Exactly how many Death Notes are there in the story? Who owns them and when?

O ver the course of the story, four Death Notes appear in the human world. Since each shinigami gets one Death Note, we can conveniently call them "Ryuk's," "Rem's," "Jealous's," and "Sidoh's."

Ryuk carries his Death Note at his side throughout the story and it isn't seen used until he kills Light with it at the end. No human ever touches it.

The first one to be used by humans, that is, Light, is Sidoh's. Sidoh drops his by accident, and Ryuk picks it up, fools the shinigami king, and puts it in the human world with his own written instructions on how to use it, written in English, the most common human language, to see what will happen. Light picks it up. Since he's the first human to touch it, he becomes its owner. Since Ryuk was the one who brought it to the human world, he's the one responsible for haunting its owner and he's the shinigami Light can see.

As part of a plan, Light gives up Sidoh's Death Note and has Ryuk give it to Rem. For a short period, the notebook once again has no human owner. It's just Rem's. Rem lets Higuchi pick it up. Then Higuchi becomes its owner, with Rem haunting him. When Higuchi dies and L, Light, and the police take the Death Note, they give it to Light's father to hide. It's not clear who the owner is at that point. Then, when Rem dies, it stops having a shinigami overseer.

The mafia led by Mello takes Sidoh's Death Note from the police in exchange for the hostage the mafia kidnaps — Light's little sister, Sayu. Meanwhile, from the shinigami world, Sidoh realizes where he lost the Death Note. Sidoh tries to get Ryuk to give him back his Death Note, but Ryuk isn't the one in charge of it anymore. He gave it to Rem, who's now dead, which means no shinigami is in charge of it. Sidoh's options are to hang around the human owner of the Death Note until the human dies and then grab it before some other human does or get the Death Note willingly returned by the owner. The owner turns out to be Kal Snydar, one of the mafia members. So Sidoh helps Snydar and the mafia kill the police Light sends to get the Death Note back. This clearly seems to be an instance of a shinigami saving the lives of particular humans, but Sidoh doesn't die, probably because the rule against this only applies to shinigami's use of the Death Note. Eventually, Sidoh gets his Death Note back and returns to the shinigami world with it. That's the last that's seen or heard of Sidoh's Death Note.

Jealous's notebook is used by Jealous to lengthen Misa's life, which kills him. Rem takes it and gives it to Misa, its first human owner in the story. Rem then haunts Misa. L captures and imprisons Misa. Rem saves Misa by having her give up her Death Note. At the time, Light is the one in physical possession of Jealous's Death Note, so he becomes the new owner. Light has Rem trade it with Ryuk for Sidoh's Death Note, gives up Sidoh's Death Note, and becomes the owner only of Jealous's Death Note under the aegis of Ryuk instead of Rem. He then buries Jealous's Death Note, and, while he is in prison, he surrenders ownership of it, leaving it without a human owner. Later, under Light's directions, Misa digs up Jealous's Death Note, once again becoming its owner and overseen by Ryuk. Light takes the Death Note without taking over Misa's ownership, hides it under his clothes, and resumes his criminal-killing activities as Kira. Late in the story, he has Misa give it to Teru Mikami, letting him be the new owner. Mikami then does Kira's killing. That makes Ryuk responsible for haunting Mikami, but he already has to watch over Rem's Death Note with the police, so he can't always be with Mikami. Near secretly seizes Jealous's Death Note from Mikami, tricks Light into exposing himself as Kira, and burns it.

Rem's Death Note stays with her for a long time as she guards Misa. She uses it to save Misa and dies, leaving it for Light to pick up, becoming its new owner with no attached shinigami. He uses this for his activities as Kira while Sidoh's is guarded by the police. In order to get Sidoh's Death Note back from Mello, he gives up ownership of Rem's notebook and sends it to the police. His father becomes the new owner, haunted by Ryuk, and makes the bargain for shinigami eyes with Ryuk. When Light's father dies, the ownership goes back to Light, although the police keep the Death Note itself in a safe. In the final showdown, Aizawa takes it to the Yellow

Box, and, in the end, Near burns it.

19 How much does one forget when one loses ownership of the Death Note?

Someone who has gained ownership of and used the Death Note and then loses ownership will lose all of his or her memories related to the Death Note, while any memories not related to the Death Note will remain. When Misa is imprisoned by L as a second Kira suspect, she surrenders her ownership of the Death Note at Rem's suggestion and thereby loses her memories of it. Consequently, she no longer remembers why she is imprisoned. Similarly, Light actually plans to be imprisoned, surrenders his ownership of the Death Note, and loses his memories.

In Misa's case, before she lost her memory, she found out about the Death Note and used it to find Kira (Light). After she surrenders her Death Note, she no longer remembers that Light is Kira or how it is that she met him (apparently, she concludes that she went to Aoyama for no particular reason, just happened to see him, and fell in love at first sight).

Light does remember that he asked L to imprison him (although that was originally part of his plan as Kira), but he doesn't remember that he was Kira. Because of this, until he gets his memory back, he makes a serious effort with L to catch Kira.

Since his experiences with the Death Note are longer than

Misa's, inconsistencies occur in Light's memories of his past. One subtle example is that Light apparently forgets that he rode the Yamanote Line with FBI agent Raye Penber, even though that's a pretty substantial fact that would have evidence of it occurring. More critically, Light should remember having put a small television in a bag of potato chips in order to watch the news while making it appear to the hidden cameras in his room that he wasn't. Of course, he forgets the situation, but putting the television in the chip bag wasn't directly connected to the Death Note, as Misa's going to Aoyama or her love for Light aren't. However, if he does remember the small television, this should make him suspicious. Since he's forgotten about the Death Note and is seriously trying to find Kira with L, surely he should immediately believe that he has been manipulated by Kira and strongly assert the likelihood of such to L, instead of vaguely thinking that he might have been manipulated.

Apparently, Misa only forgets memories directly related to the Death Note, but Light forgets everything that doesn't make sense without the Death Note memories. Therefore, it seems that what memories are lost depends on the individual.

20 Are all of the rules of the Death Note explained?

From the beginning, Ryuk says that even shinigami don't know all the rules and that they don't have to explain all the rules to humans. Also, Ryuk is willing to write false rules for the Death Note. If that's true, then there's no way of knowing whether every rule he tells Light is necessarily true. Sidoh, the shinigami who comes to get his Death Note back, knows very little about the rules and gets a book about them from Armonia Jastin Beyondllemason, said to be the shinigami's "answergod." It looks like shinigami who know all the rules are rare. Perhaps the situation is that, since the shinigami world has become such a lazy place and the shinigami never strain themselves in their use of their Death Notes, the current shinigami have no motivation to learn all the details. Even Rem, who seems more serious than most of the shinigami, only teaches Misa the basic rules. Misa doesn't learn that one can kill with a scrap of the Death Note until Light teaches her.

Even when Ryuk explains rules, he doesn't even consistently seem sure that he is right, especially in the rules concerning shinigami, such as the one against shinigami telling humans about the presence of other shinigami.

The sources of Light's knowledge of the rules are Ryuk and

his own experiments. It is likely that there are rules that Ryuk never tells him and Light never discovers.

21 When did a Death Note previously come to the human world?

When Light and Ryuk first meet, Ryuk says that Death Notes have circulated in the human world before, but doesn't explain when.

It's not certain when the system of the Death Note, taking human life by writing down names, was first established, but let's suppose it existed at the birth of the human race. In that case, humans hadn't yet invented writing, so, even if the Death Note fell into the human world, humans wouldn't be able to use it. Even after writing was invented, people didn't meet all the requirements, such as having a full name, legal name, and true name, incorporated into the Death Note rules. It seems that the Death Note may be a fairly recent invention. Even now, in fact, there are societies that lack writing systems and have names that change as they grow up.

Ryuk says that the Death Note was used by humans before, but that Light is the first human he knows of who has killed so many people in so short a time. The last time, then, must have been at a time when humans had the ability to handle the Death Note, maybe a few hundred years ago. However, since there isn't any remaining sign of its last use, it couldn't have been as dramatic as Light's.

22 Is it impossible to kill someone indirectly with the Death Note?

I t is possible to manipulate someone's actions before death by writing them into the description of the conditions of death. If one just writes a name and doesn't write anything else for 40 seconds, the victim will die of a heart attack. But if one writes in a cause of death before that (such as "dies in an accident"), one has six minutes and 40 seconds to specify the details of the situation. Thus, one can, for example, write, "Commits suicide after writing his name on the wall," and make the victim do it.

However, one can't write "Commits suicide after killing X" —the Death Note can't make a victim kill another person. This makes sense, since the Death Note is a tool for shinigami to acquire human life spans and add them to their own. Not only would there be no point in having a human kill another human, but it would be a waste of a life that the shinigami could take. A shinigami should just write both humans in the Death Note, separately, in order to directly kill both of them and gain their lives. Thus, one can't make humans kill other humans with the Death Note. Another implication of this is that one can't, for example, write of a pilot of a passenger aircraft, "Dies of a heart attack while flying," because the pilot's death would kill all the passengers. If the pilot died, it would have to be after he has landed, when it would not kill anyone else.

Light obviously has a very thorough understanding of the rules when he kills the twelve FBI agents. First, since he knows Raye Penber's name and face, he writes of him, "December 27, 2003, brings his computer, passes the cafe "cafeel" in Shinjuku, gets on the Yamanote Line, and dies three seconds after getting off." Then, by direct intimidation, not by using the Death Note, he makes Penber get a file with the names and faces of all the FBI agents who have entered Japan onto his computer. Finally, he has Penber write down their names on what is actually paper torn out from the Death Note with the hidden words, "After receiving a file about the FBI agents, dies at" a certain time. From Light's point of view, he uses the Death Note indirectly to kill the rest of the FBI agents, but, from the Death Note's point of view, Penber kills them directly. It works.

23 Is it impossible to lengthen someone's life with the Death Note?

The Death Note can only manipulate the circumstances of death up to 23 days after the name is written. This generally means that anyone whose name is written in the Death Note will die within 23 days. One can't effectively write, "Dies in 53 years." The exception is if one writes "dies from disease." In that case, if one just writes that and the name of a disease that would take three years to kill the victim, it will kill the victim in three years. However, if one writes the name of a disease that couldn't kill the victim before the victim was going to die already, the victim would just die of a heart attack.

Humans' life spans are decided by fate. If someone is already fated to die in 12 days, it's meaningless to write in the Death Note, "Dies after 13 days." Jealous, however, lengthens Misa's life span by killing the stalker who was fated to stab her to death. This would seem likely to result in Misa having a heart attack before she was stabbed. However, his purpose is to lengthen Misa's life. The remaining life that was supposed to be his ends up going to her. Even though the basic purpose of shinigami is to take human life, clearly, it is possible for them to give their own lives to humans.

Humans, unlike shinigami, do not receive the life they take

from others with the Death Note, but, in exchange, they are able to kill people in order to extend other lives without dying or receiving any other penalty. Only with a Death Note can humans change fate.

So, it's impossible to lengthen someone's life directly with the Death Note (by writing that they should live longer), but it can be possible to indirectly lengthen someone's life with it, if one kills a prospective killer.

24 What happens when a human uses the Death Note without owning it?

A human can use the Death Note whether they own it or not. In fact, the FBI agent Raye Penber uses it to successfully kill despite not knowing that he is using a Death Note, not even knowing what a Death Note is or that they exist, not intending to kill, just because he does, in fact, write the names of the other FBI agents on the paper of Light's Death Note while thinking of their faces.

Non-owners actually have a lot of advantages over owners. Touching a Death Note that one doesn't own allows one to see the shinigami associated with it, even after one lets go of the Death Note. When the actual owner of the Death Note loses ownership, that person stops being able to see the shinigami and forgets about the Death Note. However, non-owners remember everything. The shinigami only stalks the owner, because, when the owner dies, the shinigami needs to write his or her name in the shinigami's own notebook (to turn that person into a shinigami, possibly). Those who are just borrowing the Death Note aren't stalked by any shinigami and don't have to become shinigami after they die.

Chapter 03

Light's Secrets

25 Is Light right in what he does?

Light intends use the Death Note to punish criminals, reduce crime, and eventually create an ideal, crime-free world with himself as its god. This is referred to in Death Note as "Kira philosophy," after "Kira," the name given to the godlike figure who metes out punishment to the evil, even causing one prisoner after another to die of a sudden heart attack while in jail and totally isolated. ("Kira," by the way, is said in the story to come from the English "Killer," but it also means "Sparkle" in Japanese, appropriate for someone named Light, as well as for the police's sparkly Kira logo they use when they respond to Misa as Kira.)

Light manages to reduce the global crime rate by 70 percent, stop war, and gain the cooperation of various countries including the United States, although the latter simply gives up opposing Kira. Light's ideal world never has a chance to come to full fruition because of his death. However, when Death Note came to a close, there was enormous controversy on Japanese Internet forums over the Kira philosophy, with people saying, "If he hadn't died, would he have been able to create the perfect world?" "Wasn't he right after all?" "No, he was wrong," etc. The question that arises is how it would have been if he hadn't died.

It is true that Light manages to reduce crime drastically and eventually win mass support, so he may have been right in some senses. But let's think about what would happen if we applied his philosophy in the real world. All Light knows about the criminals is what the media tells him. Normally, these criminals would mostly be caught and arrested by the police. Then they would have a trial by jury, investigating whether there was really enough evidence to conclude that they were truly guilty. Some of them would be found not guilty as charged. Those who were found guilty would have the circumstances taken into consideration and given a sentence considered appropriate to the crime. Light, however, kills mostly people who have been accused but not convicted. He probably kills many people who were actually innocent, perhaps even framed.

Light also kills a number of people who aren't criminals, simply to guard himself, like the FBI agents looking for him, Naomi Misora (the fiancée of one of the FBI agents), and Kiyomi Takada (who is on his side!). If there were another powerful Kira, Light would likely be judged as one of the criminals who should be punished. But, in the ideal world of Light's Kira philosophy, Light is beyond judgment or punishment. He can get away with anything while everyone else can get away with nothing. This is dangerous. A safe, fair society needs judges even for those who judge.

26 Does Light really believe that he can bring about an ideal world?

When Light first picks up the Death Note, he doesn't think it will actually work, but chooses Kuro Otoharada, a murderer he sees on the news, to try it out so as not to feel guilty if it does work. When it does work, he does feel guilty. To justify his actions, he tells himself that evil criminals are better off dead. But that's not enough to rid him of his sense of guilt. So he then decides that, in fact, criminals should die, and it is necessary to kill them all in order to create an ideal society. The true origin of Kira thinking, then, is as a way for Light to feel less guilty. He goes on to kill so many people in the five days before he meets Ryuk that even Ryuk, a god of death, is amazed. By this point, Light has to create the ideal society, or he'll end up nothing more than a mass murderer. So the Kira philosophy snowballs from Light's attempt to justify his killing of Kuro Otoharada.

When Light loses his memory of being Kira from the time L imprisons him to the time they catch Higuchi, he hates Kira with all his heart and puts all his efforts into trying to catch Kira. This is strong evidence that Light doesn't originally believe in the Kira philosophy.

L ight appears to kill over a hundred criminals in one week after getting the Death Note. Police worldwide can't help but notice this. There's no way so many criminals could have heart attacks within such a short time frame. But, since the Death Note is a tool of the shinigami world and is unknown amongst humans, this is not recognized at first as being the work of another criminal. Light feels even more confident because he's seen as such an outstanding student; he feels he is the only one who can put the Death Note to good use; he is arrogant.

But then the world's greatest detective, L, figures out this phenomenon is human-created, that there's someone killing all these criminals, and that someone is in Japan. Light must be pretty shocked to realize that someone can figure all this out when he's using a weapon that, to all normal earthly appearances, appears to be miraculous. And then L accuses Light of being evil. For Light, who now sees himself as the justice of the world, being accused in such a way is the greatest humiliation imaginable.

Still trusting in the invincibility of his divine Death Note, Light tries to kill L. But this is exactly what L is expecting. For if Light were truly just, he would ignore L's challenge and proceed in his spree of killing criminals. As soon as he tries to kill L, his claims to justice crumble. From then to the very end, Light continues on a path that others see as simply evil.

28 Does Light care about his family?

Light lives in a family of four: his father Soichiro, who works for the police, his mother Sachiko, his little sister Sayu, and himself. Sayu is proud of her brother, the outstanding student, while Light looks up to his father. From the beginning, Light wants to follow his father into the police force, which he eventually does. It seems to be, at least at first, a loving household with no particular problems.

When Sayu is kidnapped, Light is concerned about her rescue. However, he looks down on his honest, hardworking father and behaves somewhat coldly when he dies. He even shows signs that he's willing to kill his family if necessary, even very soon after he gets the Death Note. He says to Ryuk, "If my sister saw you, that would probably be enough to give her a heart attack." This line is famous among some readers, who believe that Light means, "If my sister saw you, I wouldn't even need to write her name in the Death Note, because she would die of a heart attack anyway."

Light also has a lot of girlfriends during the course of the story, such as Yuri, Kiyomi Takada and Misa, but he never treats them as anything but tools, and he never shows any sign that he actually loves them. To the very end, Light doesn't seem to truly love anyone, whether it's his family or his girlfriend. He only seems to love himself. He doesn't believe there are many people in the world that he can rely on. He can be described as an extreme narcissist.

29 Was it really necessary for Light to kill all the FBI agents?

After Light receives L's challenge, he comes to the conclusion that it's not enough just to hide. He has to find L himself and kill him. Light intentionally leaks to L the fact that information is leaking from the police to Kira. This makes L cast suspicion on those associated with the police, but that in turn causes the police to look suspiciously at L, a person associated with the police but who investigates while hiding his own identity. Most of the police on the case resign.

Within this context, the FBI, at L's command, gets closer to Light. Light seems a bit nervous, but he can't just kill the agent who's investigating him, or those suspicious of him will become even more so. If he is going to kill him, he needs to kill all the FBI agents who have come to Japan. But even having the Death Note doesn't make such a task simple. It seems Light could just lie low until the threat passes—there's no way they could find out that he has a Death Note in his room he's using to kill. But he decides to kill them anyhow.

The reasons are that, this way, L will no longer be able to get help from the FBI, and, also, it will be brought to light that they were investigating the police's families, which deepens the police's mistrust of L, finally forcing L to show his face.

Light uses the Death Note to make the drug addict Kiichiro Osoreda hijack a bus he's on, gets the FBI agent trailing him to show his name Raye Penber on his FBI ID to him, and, through further clever use of the Death Note, manages to exploit Penber to kill all twelve of the FBI, making the ground under L, who brought the FBI to Japan, even shakier. The Japanese police realize that Kira will kill anyone who tries to catch him; most of the police are frightened off, leaving the investigation with only six members.

Meanwhile, L has to show his face. Light's plan is all almost perfect. The one problem is that it helps L track him down. Before, L knew only that Kira was in Japan. Now, he realizes that Kira must be somewhere in the area, and among the people the FBI were investigating. L gets ever closer.

When Ryuk alerts Light to the fact that someone is tailing him, Light is able to figure out that L believes Kira is connected to the police and that he has put the families of the police under surveillance. He wants to find out who it is that L sent. This is where the bus-jacking incident comes in. It's a strategy Light devises to give them a reason to look in the face of his shadower and find out his name, so that he'll be able to kill him with the Death Note. He picks out Kiichiro Osoreda, a criminal drug addict, to spearhead his plan. He writes his name in the Death Note, and continues:

December 20, 2003 (Saturday)

Leaves at 11:31 a.m. from the bus stop at the east gate of the park at Hanazono-ku, 3-chome,

boards the South-North Spaceland-bound bus with a pistol loaded with six bullets,

takes the passengers hostage,

tries to steal cash from the driver,

then sees a frightening vision not of this world,

fires all of his bullets at it,

runs away for fear and lack of bullets,

gets off the bus,

and dies there in an accident at 11:45 a.m.

What is interesting about this tactic is the kind of prediction of the future it allows. Two people know what Osoreda is going to do: Osoreda and Light. Light uses the Death Note, almost like a crystal ball.

But only Osoreda knows for sure exactly what Osoreda is going to do—there is leeway within Light's description that might allow Osoreda to upset his plan. Light knows much less what Penber, the FBI agent, and Yuri, the girl he brings along to further his plan, are going to do. He may have expectations, but there is a limit to what it's possible for him to predict, and there are many things that could go wrong.

For instance, if Yuri is late for their date, the plan won't work; if Penber doesn't sit in the seat behind him, it won't work; if Penber doesn't notice the note he shows to Yuri and stop Light from attacking Osoreda, it won't work; and if Penber doesn't show Light his FBI ID, it won't work. None of these are sure bets. Putting all these together, it seems extremely unlikely that Light's plan, in the end, would work. Yet it does.

W hen everyone involved in the official Kira investigation, including L, still thinks heart attacks are the only way Kira kills, Naomi Misora, the fiancée of FBI agent Raye Penber until he is killed by Kira, realizes that Kira can kill in other ways. She knows about the Shinjuku bus-jacking incident in which Penber showed his FBI identification to one of the other passengers, and thinks that this is the only opportunity Kira could have had to find out about the FBI. The hijacker died when he was hit by a car, not by a heart attack, and so the police and L didn't make any connection with Kira. But that makes it all the more reasonable to Naomi that the incident was planned by Kira to find out about the FBI.

This leads her to the conclusion that Kira must be able to kill by means other than heart attacks. Naomi heads to the police to tell them of her discovery. Light will be the first person to fall under scrutiny. All the investigators know that Penber was the one investigating the Yagami family.

Naomi, by bad luck, runs into Light before she gets the chance to speak with the police. She explains her reasoning to him, and he writes her name in the Death Note. But her death is never shown, leading fans for a long time to speculate that she was still alive.

Naomi is the first bystander Light kills on impulse. So far, he has only killed criminals and FBI agents. The FBI killings were part of a careful plan to isolate L, whereas he kills Naomi seemingly just for coming too close to the truth. Thus, many fans claimed that "Even under Kira philosophy, that's not enough justification to kill her," and, "Naomi's not really dead; she'll come back sometime late in the story."

But her name is in the Death Note. How could she survive?

There are possible theories. First, perhaps Naomi Misora isn't her real name—she was cautious enough not only to tell Light a fake name originally, but also to use a false name on her ID. She used to be an FBI agent herself, after all. Another theory is that she's pregnant and therefore protected by the rule that the Death Note cannot kill in ways that indirectly kill others (in this case, her baby). In the end, however, Naomi doesn't appear again, so these theories are unlikely. But they are still possible.

32 Why doesn't Light ever make the deal for shinigami eyes?

When Light realizes that there's someone, Penber, tailing him and considers how he could find out the person's name, Ryuk suggests that he make the bargain for shinigami eyes. But Light refuses, and in fact never accepts.

To acquire shinigami eyes, which would enable him to see people's names, Light would have to relinquish to Ryuk half of his remaining life. Light says he doesn't want to do this because his shortened life might not be long enough to create the perfect world. But is this really the reason?

It is more plausible that Light simply hates the thought of having to sacrifice anything to get what he wants. He kills and kills without hesitation with the Death Note because it doesn't seem to cost him anything.

Another reason he doesn't make the deal is because of his conceited belief in his own intelligence. He believes that his brain more than outweighs any benefit he would gain from having shinigami eyes. (He turns out to overestimate himself.) However, he is all too happy to make aggressive use of others who can use the eyes for him, such as Misa and Mikami. Light's father sacrifices half his remaining life to get the eyes, feeling responsible for having put the Death Note in the hands of mafia, despite his duty as a police officer. Even then, when it comes time, he can't bring himself to make use of them to kill Mello.

Light wants to be heralded as a god without having to make sacrifices. He wants it all, and he thinks he can get it.

33 When does Light put the TV in the potato chips bag?

After FBI agent Raye Penber's fiancée Naomi Misora disappears, L's suspicions fall on the families that Penber was investigating. He decides to investigate them himself and places hidden cameras in their houses, including Light's. Light, however, is a step ahead. Using a miniature television and a scrap of the Death Note hidden in a bag of potato chips, he continues his Kira killings.

The cameras are placed on January 8. The same day, Light immediately recognizes that someone has entered his room. He has Ryuk search for hidden cameras. Light goes outside and buys a porno magazine to provide an excuse for why he put a card in his door to check for intruders. Then, that night, he kills using the miniature television and scrap of the Death Note hidden in a chips bag placed on his study desk so that the cameras can't see inside.

But when does he prepare the TV chip bag? If it were after he realizes cameras have been installed, he wouldn't be able to do it in the house, because he would be caught on the cameras. Doing it when he went out to buy the magazine is not an option, because when he comes home, all he's carrying is the magazine bag.

Therefore, he must have prepared the bag well in advance,

predicting that his room might someday be bugged. He used consommé-flavor chips, which he knew no one in his family would eat. This allowed him to leave the bag in the cupboard without his family noticing that there was a television inside. It is clear that his family uses this cupboard. If someone else were to take out the chips by mistake, they would certainly feel that there was something heavy inside. That would take some explaining. In conclusion, this is another of Light's many plans that work largely through sheer luck.

Why does Light have Ryuk and Rem exchange Death Notes before he is imprisoned?

When Misa is imprisoned and the secrets of the Death Note seem on the verge of being exposed, Light devises a plan in which he is imprisoned and Ryuk and Rem exchange Death Notes.

Here is Light's reasoning. Misa was using Jealous' Death Note, haunted by Rem. If Light just buried Jealous's Death Note with Rem still associated with it, Rem would end up being the one to haunt Misa again. But Rem is protective of Misa. When Misa gives up her ownership the first time, she also loses her shinigami eyes; Light is going to want her to get new ones, but Rem might refuse to take half of Misa's life again. If Light buries Sidoh's Death Note (the one Light originally found) instead, then, when Misa digs it up, it would be Ryuk that would haunt her. If Misa doesn't get back the ownership of Jealous's Death Note, the one she was using before, she will never regain her memories.

Light's plan is for a new Kira (who ends up being Higuchi) to emerge and for L and himself to track down the new Kira, believing he will touch the Death Note again and all his memories will return. For that to work, it has to be Sidoh's Death Note, the one Light owned before. Light's solution is to have Ryuk and Rem trade Death Notes, so that Rem will follow Sidoh's notebook and Ryuk will follow Jealous's. Light goes into prison with ownership of Jealous's notebook, but then surrenders his ownership, and therefore his memories.

35 Why does Light have Ryuk write false rules in the Death Note?

L
ight is able to temporarily lift the suspicion on him when he asks to be imprisoned and gives up the ownership of the Death Note. He is able to predict that, in the course of his search for Kira, L will find out about the Death Note. Even after Light's imprisonment, L will continue to suspect Light, realize that Kira's power may be able to change hands, and suspect Light of giving it to someone else. For L, the possibilities would be either that an outside Kira manipulated both Light and Higuchi or that Light is Kira.

A problem for Light is that he kept his Kira powers until the last minute. This would suggest that Light is Kira; otherwise, Kira would be expected to have transferred his power away from Light to someone else before Light was questioned more thoroughly. L's suspicion of Light only deepens when he finds the Death Note and sees that the power can, in fact, change owners.

So Light has Ryuk write in the Death Note the lie, "If the person using the note fails to consecutively write names of people to be killed within 13 days of each other, then the user will die." This gives Light a firm alibi. L sees for himself that Light went for more than 13 days in prison without using a

Death Note. According to the fake rule, if he were Kira, he would be dead. This is very effective at getting L off Light's back.

Light also has Ryuk write, "If you make this Death Note unusable by tearing it up or burning it, all the humans who have touched the note till then will die." This way, even if L and the police get their hands on the Death Note, they won't destroy it.

36 Why does Rem have to kill L and Watari?

Light's plan to get back the Death Note works, and he and Misa return to their previous positions as Kira and "the second Kira." To the general public, it looks as if the Kira killings have gone on uninterrupted, since Misa resumes them immediately after Higuchi dies. But L is aware that they're resuming, not merely continuing, with perfect timing, which puts Misa once again under suspicion. Yet even this is part of Light's plan.

Rem is protective of Misa, the human another shinigami, Jealous, cared for so dearly that he gave his life for her. When Rem first realizes that Light is using Misa, she seems rather unnerved and angered. But, after following Higuchi and coming to despise humans for their avarice and sleaze, she starts to sympathize with Light and his wish to make the world better. One might even say she likes him. If all she cared about was saving Misa, she could wait things out a little longer and still be able to save Misa when it indeed proves necessary. But L suspects Light, too. Because Rem cares for both Light and Misa, she decides that she has to get rid of L and Watari. For this, she gives up her life.

Light really knows what he's doing. He even understands Rem's psyche, and he is able to play her like his checkmate piece in his chess game against L.

37 Why does Light take over L's name when L dies?

From the police's point of view, it makes perfect sense: Light has been part of the Kira investigation under L since the early days, and he has consistently shown himself the only one to rival L in deductive power. In any case, when L dies, they wouldn't want Kira or the public to know about it; someone has to substitute for L.

Light doesn't even have to bring it up himself; others make his case for him. Light doesn't refuse because that's what he's been planning all along.

It's ideal for Light. On the surface, he's the head of the investigation to find Kira. Within, he is Kira. An investigation run by the one it is investigating is highly unlikely ever to succeed. Light knows for a fact what Kira is doing, making it very easy for him to follow him. He probably anticipates hearing the public say, "L is amazing, but Kira is something else." And, even if the other investigators start to catch on to the fact that Light is actually Kira, he can spin them off in the wrong direction with ease.

38 How does Light take his father's death?

L ight's plan, originally, when he and the police work
out how they're going to invade Mello's hideout and
get the Death Note back, is that Matsuda will make
the bargain for the shinigami eyes, they'll get the Death Note
from Mello, and Matsuda will write Mello's name in the Death
Note.

However, Light's father, Soichiro, feels responsible for
having given the Death Note to Mello and asks to be the one
to make the bargain. He's no longer young. If he gives away
half of his life, he can be expected not to have too long to live.
But no one can refuse his offer because he has a strong belief
in duty. Indeed, he dies in a hospital soon after the police
operation.

Even at his deathbed, Light's attention is focused on
getting him to write Mello's name in the Death Note. Since
other members of the investigation are also in the room, Light
pretends to be caring for his father. But he actually considers
Mello's death a higher priority than the life of his father.

When Soichiro dies without writing any name in the
notebook, Light acts as if he's for grieving his father, but it
seems he struggling to control his anger. At the end, when the
investigators discover that Light is Kira, Matsuda confronts

him over his father's death. But Light declares that Soichiro had to die in order to build the ideal society.

The fact that Light is even willing to sacrifice his family for an ideal shows that he has become a shinigami. In the beginning, Light respects his father and studies hard to become a policeman like him; it is clear that he truly loves him. The Death Note changes Light's personality.

39 Why does Light give his Death Note to Teru Mikami?

After the incident in which Mello kidnaps Sayu and steals the Death Note, Near, L's true successor, begins to suspect Light is Kira. His logic is so persuasive that it gets Light worried. Light figures that the weakest link through which the truth is likely to escape is Misa, and so he has to have her give up her Death Note so that no one will be able to find any proof even if they investigate her. But Light is always holed up in the Kira investigation office leading the team as L, and under suspicion; he doesn't have the time or opportunity to write Kira's targets in the Death Note himself. He needs a new second Kira.

It might be possible for Light to take Misa's ownership of Jealous's notebook. But that would be limited to 490 days, if he lent it to Mikami, because the rules say that, after that period of time, ownership transfers to the borrower. It looks like Light might have to leave it with Mikami for longer.

Also, according to Light's plans, the second Kira needs to have shinigami eyes. Light can have Mikami make the bargain, but, to do that, Mikami needs to own the Death Note. Normally, this would mean that Ryuk would have to be with Mikami. However, Ryuk has to supervise Rem's Death Note at the investigation headquarters with Light, leaving it up to

Ryuk to decide where to be. Light realizes how convenient this all is and gives Mikami ownership of the Death Note.

40 Why does Light, in the end, fail?

When Near challenges Light, telling him he'll finally prove he is Kira, Light guesses that Near's plan involves the Death Note.

The only way Near could prove that Light is Kira is by catching him in the act of writing in the Death Note or by getting the second Kira to write in the Death Note in a particular way that would prove that Light was Kira. Since Near specifies where and when he'll prove who is Kira, Light speculates that Near is planning to have the second Kira write in the Death Note. In that case, Near must be planning to do something to Mikami's notebook.

Light has a good track record of staying one step ahead of his opponent. Now that he has figured out this much, a safe strategy would be to postpone the meeting and see how Near reacts. But Light overestimates his own intelligence. He wants to show Near up, and then bring him down. He replaces Mikami's Death Note with a fake and awaits victory. However, things turn out quite different. When Mello kidnaps Kiyomi Takada, Mikami uses his real Death Note in order to kill Takada, alerting Near to Light's plan.

Despite this, Light is still convinced that he's won; so much that he declares victory before its been called. It's already too late when realizes that's he's all but confessed.

In fact, when one looks back objectively, there are numerous flaws in Light's strategy, beginning with when he killed the FBI agents. The fact that he assumes everyone will do what he thinks they will is one of such flaws. For much of the story, his plans succeed. But when it comes to the end, his assumptions of what Mello and Mikami will do or not do turn out to be wrong, and everything falls apart. A truly wise tactician is one who accounts for the fact that others may not act as expected and devises a complete strategy that will succeed regardless.

Even the "Kira philosophy" – showing the world what is right by sentencing to death those who transgress societies rules—is based on Light's assumptions about people's wants and needs. It is based on these assumptions that the killing spree begins. But no one can predict the thoughts and actions of others.

Light is doomed to fail because he is too self-interested.

Column 02

Death Note Movies

After the success of the manga and anime, Death Note was made into a live-action movie. The original production plan called for a single two-hour movie. However, the makers decided to split the film into two at the last minute, and Death Note became the first Japanese movie in history to have two volumes playing simultaneously. With both parts combined, its box office receipts totaled a spectacular 8 billion yen (about 66 million dollars).

The director, Shusuke Kaneko, is renowned for his science fiction films, which include the 1995 Gamera: Guardian of the Universe, rated one of Japan's top 10 movies ever, and the 1996 Gamera 2: The Attack of Legion, which won the 17th Japanese Science Fiction Award.

Once it was decided to split the movie into two parts, it became necessary to make major changes to the script. Caught under an avalanche of work and an impending deadline, screenwriter Tetsuya Oishi struggled to make the changes, leaving the production team to consider returning to a single-volume format.

But Kaneko decided to stick with two volumes, assistant director Yoshinori Matsugae helped make a polished final script faithful to Oishi's original draft, and they managed to shoot the movie without further hitch.

The movie version is based on the first seven volumes of the manga, and therefore it has its own, very different ending, in which L finally discovers that Light is Kira.

Volume I

1. Light is a To-Oh University student who passed the bar exam on his first try.
2. L is an "unknown person sent by the ICPO to Tokyo."
3. The Japanese-American FBI agent is named Raye Iwamatsu, not Raye Penber. All main characters are played by Japanese actors.
4. There are two new characters: Shiori Akino is Light's childhood friend and in the same year as him at To-Oh University; Sawa is a female detective in the central Kira investigation. The detective Ide, on the other hand, does not appear.

Volume II

1. Kiyomi Takada works for Sakura TV, not NHN.
2. Takada doesn't know Light, and she is older.
3. There are two other new characters: Saeko Nishiyama is a top newscaster at Sakura TV; and Ayako Yoshino is another employee.
4. The Yotsuba Group, Aiber and Wedy do not appear.
5. Demegawa's first name is changed from Hitoshi to Hiroshi.
6. Ukita and Mogi have their names switched.
7. Soichiro Yagami, instead of being the police investigation bureau chief, is the police investigation department chief.

Chapter 04

L's Secrets

In one week, some 100 criminals around the world die of heart attacks. It is the beginning of what will later be called the "Kira case."

The ICPO (Interpol) cannot figure out whether this is a coincidence or the work of organized crime. It has no idea who might the culprit be, why they would do it, and how they could do it. What they know is that within a week over 100 criminals in prison or on the run died of heart attacks. It is time for L, the genius detective who has solved so many of the world's thorniest cases in the past, to step forward.

L investigates the over 100 dead and observes a pattern. The ones who are dying are mostly infamous criminals whose cases are widely covered in the media. These are not death-row criminals, to whom media access is restricted. This proves that the culprit is human, and not some divine force to which media attention would be of no concern. Furthermore, because the dead are generally not politically affiliated, L can deduce that the perpetrator's power does not involve power or money. Combined with the limits of the perpetrator's information, this clue suggests that the one behind the deaths is an average Joe.

Also, as the deaths started so suddenly, it seems likely that the perpetrator has only recently gained the power. Therefore,

L searches for a harbinger incident before the deaths started en masse and finds the isolated, unusual incident of Kuro Otoharada, a murderer and street thug. As L further checks his supposition that the perpetrator lives in Japan, he finds that the victims are mostly criminals made public by the media in Japan. The number of Japanese criminals is disproportionately skewed.

At this point, L still hasn't determined for a fact that someone in Japan is killing the criminals, but his reasoning nevertheless takes him quite far.

42 Why does L make the live broadcast in which he challenges Kira?

Not only does L figure that the killer is Japanese, but he also notices that some of the worst criminals aren't the ones dying. He notes that all those who have died have something in common: they've all had their names and faces shown publicly. So L speculates that Kira can't kill without knowing his victim's name and face. He wants to test his suppositions, and he does this by challenging Kira in a live broadcast.

His real motive is to find out Kira's location and method of killing. Because of the criminal in Japan who died of a heart attack shortly before the mass deaths started was a very minor one whose case would have only been publicized in the Kanto region, L guesses that Kira is in ordinary civilian resident of Kanto. L launches his experiment from that standpoint.

He takes on a confrontational attitude as he says on TV, "Kill me!" However, what he's really concerned about is whether and when Lind L. Tailor, a criminal already sentenced to death he's put in his place, will die. He has to motivate Kira to action or the experiment will be meaningless.

If Tailor doesn't die, it will increase the probability that either Kira needs more than a name and face to kill or that Kira doesn't exist in the first place (that the phenomenon is not directly caused by a human). If Tailor dies a while after the broadcast, it will suggest that Kira needs some time to satisfy certain conditions for killing. L can also rebroadcast the show in different regions at different times if necessary, which could give a hint as to where Kira might be located. In any case, if Tailor dies, it is conclusive proof that a human is causing the heart attacks.

Light is taken in completely by L's challenge, and kills Tailor believing he's L, only to hear the real L continue to challenge him. This confirms to L that Kira exists, was watching the broadcast in the Kanto area, can kill people if he knows their name and face, and can't kill people if he doesn't.

Still, there is some possibility for error. This is because the person L put in his place was a criminal. Kira kills criminals anyway. Tailor's identity had been previously hidden, but, if Kira had somehow found it out, it is possible he could have killed Tailor by coincidence. Perhaps Kira has some method of identifying and judging people other than media reports. After all, Kira already seems superhuman. So maybe Kira found out about Tailor and killed him, by coincidence, at the same time as the broadcast.

What would have happened if Light had just ignored L's challenge? L wouldn't have the support he receives based on his hypotheses. The investigation would have likely stalled. Meanwhile, since Light's father is the head of the investigation team, Light would be able to keep ahead of L.

43 Why does L show his true self to the investigation team?

L is famous among the world's police forces, even within the ICPO, as the great, unknown detective. At the beginning of the Kira case, he gives directions to the police through a computer without actually meeting anyone in person. This is later explained by the fact that he is actually all three of the Death Note world's most famous detectives (L, Erald Coil and Danuve). This way, if someone tries to find out who he is to kill him, they will probably solicit the help of another famous detective, who is actually L himself. For L to reveal his identity puts him at a definite disadvantage.

The police are looking at him with suspicion. The FBI agents he has sent to Japan have been killed. Many in the Japanese police force realize that they could very likely be killed if they remain on the case and leave in droves. Those who are left don't feel safe anymore, being the only ones showing their faces as they battle an opponent who might be able to use their faces to kill them. L can no longer retain the trust of the police without meeting them in person.

However, this is something L has planned all along.

Let's make a timetable of the Kira case so far. Light finds the Death Note on November 28, 2003. Six days later, on December 4, the ICPO discusses the heart attacks and enlists the help of L. The next day, December 5, is the day Lind L. Tailor dies; on December 14, L sends twelve FBI agents to Japan. The agents are killed on December 27. L meets the Japanese police for the first time on December 31, and, on January 17, he takes the Center Exam to get into To-Oh University.

It then turns out that L has had a large building built in Japan for the investigation using his own funds. Therefore, he must have decided that he was going to build the investigation headquarters and show himself in person even before the FBI agents were killed on December 27. Also, he needed to arrange in advance to take the Center Exam on January 17, so he must have caught on to Light quite early.

From the start, L believes the killer is a young man living in Japan. A great detective confronts the suspect so as to study the suspect's reactions. L has planned all along to show himself before Kira. Gaining the trust of the police team is just an excuse.

What does L hope to find by putting surveillance cameras in Light's house?

Observing the strange behavior of the FBI agent Raye Penber and the disappearance of his fiancée Naomi Misora, L suspects the families Penber was investigating and decides to place surveillance cameras in Vice-Chief Kitamura's and Department Chief Yagami's houses. But what is he hoping to learn?

L wants answers to three questions:

1. Does Kira use a supernatural power to kill that would make his actions untraceable?

2. Can Kira manipulate the actions of his victims before they die?

3. Does Kira need the name and face of his victim to kill? (This is still uncertain, but it seems that there are some people Kira can't kill.)

Since L doesn't know what method Kira uses to kill, he has no way of knowing which actions are suspicious and which aren't. If he knew about the Death Note, he could demonstrate that someone was or might be Kira if they showed signs of using it, but he doesn't know about the Death Note, and so he doesn't know what to look for.

Given the assumption that Kira needs his victim's name and face to kill, from L's point of view, Light appears the least likely suspect on surveillance. This is because Light doesn't appear to have access to the news at the time immediately before Kira kills someone. To continue to suspect Light, L would be pressed to give up his theory about what Kira needs to kill. Yet L does continue to suspect Light, simply because, from the beginning, he somehow finds Light extremely suspicious. He probably expects Light to reveal to the camera how he kills.

In this case, Light pulls the wool over L's eyes. Light ends up casually throwing the miniature TV he used to trick L into the trash. If L had searched a little more thoroughly and found the TV in the trash, he would have been able to put the pieces together. This is a clear victory for Light and a failure for L.

45 Why does L have to enroll in To-Oh University?

L is suspicious about Light from very early in the Kira case. However, because L doesn't have any hard evidence against Kira—he doesn't even know how the killings are carried out—he gives conservative estimates of how likely it is that Light is Kira, like 5 percent or 7 percent. Privately, he seems to feel that the probability is much higher.

Since L does suspect Light, it is only natural for him to want to now about Light's personality. L find out that Light is one of the very top students in Japan and infers that he is full of pride. L's thinking is that if Light is confronted with a competitor, he won't be able to ignore the situation, and will have to prove himself superior. Once L is confident enough about his understanding of Light's personality, he enters To-Oh University with scores matching Light's. He even tells Light directly that he's L. Faced with someone who claims to be the central member of the investigation into Kira, someone Light knows has an intellect to match his own, Light is put on his guard.

But Light prides himself on being the greatest person in the world. L can predict that Light won't be able to resist trying to outdo him. Light will attack. Meanwhile, L will watch for Light to leave himself vulnerable.

L turns out to be right. Light can't ignore him and begins gradually to dig his own grave.

L tells Light that he thinks he might be Kira, invites him to a café, and asks for his help with the investigation. L tells Light that, in order to clear L's doubts as well as to check Light's supposed brilliance, he wants to test Light's "reasoning" (although he really means Light's reactions, not his intelligence). Light has no choice but to go along with the proposal.

Of course, Light knows that L is going to ask him about Kira and try to trip him up, so Light has to be careful. But L is also prepared.

L presents Light with photos of messages from Kira—the mysterious code writings that Kira made criminals sketch out seemingly as a challenge to L. "L, do you know" "shinigami" "eat nothing but apples." Light remembers them clearly, and the sentence they spell out. But the photos L gives him have numbers on them. When lined up in that order, they read, "L, do you know shinigami that eat nothing but apples." Apparently, L is waiting to see if Light will ignore the numbers and put the pictures together in the way Kira intended them to be.

But Light's too smart for that. What one would normally observe, after putting the photographs together by the numbers, would be that the sentence doesn't look finished. In fact, L has a fake message ready, one that says "have red hands": "L, do you know shinigami that eat nothing but apples have red hands? Only Kira would know that the fourth was a fake. In fact, Light fails to think that there may be a fourth. But, when L shows it to him, Light can't say it's fake, because it's not something he should know. L forces Light into admitting he is wrong, giving him one more piece of evidence that Light may indeed be Kira.

K ira sends his first direct message to the world through Sakura TV. But it's altogether disappointing and the tape quality is poor. From the message and its execution, L can tell that this isn't something the established Kira would do. Most of all, when the speaker kills an innocent television host to prove his identity, the action clearly violates what L has so far inferred as Kira's modus operandi. L notices these differences and concludes that this is a different type of killer.

Kira has never presented himself on television or radio before. His killing has been without fanfare. This is the first time that he seems to be trying to sell himself directly to the public. Undoubtedly, if Kira chose to take such an initiative, the results would be initially surprising. It seems unreasonable to cling to rigid expectations of how Kira would act in such a situation.

L happens to be right in guessing that it's a "second Kira" (Misa), but, given what L knows, his guess is difficult to explain as anything less than divine inspiration. Furthermore, while he is quite conservative in estimating the likelihood that Light is Kira, only at 7 percent, he claims with almost total confidence (70 percent) that the person who sent the TV message is a second Kira.

We, the viewers, know that Light is Kira, so L's inference may not come as a surprise; the Kira we know wouldn't send such a message. But, from the standpoint of the investigators, it's not even sure yet that Kira is really a person or how any person could possibly cause heart attacks in other people. To blithely conclude that multiple people are causing such heart attacks is quite a leap.

However, L must already know instinctively that Light is Kira. L always treats Light as if he is Kira. He always suggests to others that it's unlikely, yet, in his mind, Kira and Light must be one and the same. By now, he's had enough time to study Light to recognize that Light wouldn't behave in such a slovenly manner. He therefore deduces that the one who sent the TV message is a different Kira.

It's not a matter of reason. L strongly feels that Light should be Kira. He wants to believe that the one behind this new message is not the original Kira. He's come so far with his supposition of Light being Kira, that he can no longer abandon it. Even if it's a logical stretch, L wants to believe there's another Kira.

48 Why can't L let go of the idea that Light is Kira?

When L tells the other investigators that he thinks there is a second Kira, they question him as to whether his conclusion up until then could have been flawed. L says that the second Kira's way of killing is different—that this Kira, instead of needing a name and a face to kill, only requires a face, and therefore there must be more than one Kira. But he still doesn't have any proof that the first Kira actually needs both a name and a face; it's simply speculation. L is willing to ignore new facts that arise because he is so convinced that Light is Kira and unwilling to change his mind.

The other investigators are aware that L believes Light is Kira. However, since there's no hard evidence, they don't lean toward the same conclusion. L tells them he is going to have Light help with the investigation and give his opinion as to what's going on. He claims that if Light suggests that there's a second Kira without any prompting from L, this will strongly suggest that Light isn't Kira.

Indeed, when Light comes to the headquarters and L explains, Light says that there must be a second Kira. For Light, this is part of his plan of staying one step ahead of L. Light surmises that if he tells the truth, it appear less likely that he is Kira. But L never stops suspecting Light, regardless of how much logical support Light seems to lend to uncovering Kira.

It's not a matter of whether L can give specific reasons why Light is likely to be Kira. L has a detective's intuition, and alarm bells ring whenever he deals with Light. As head of the investigation, he is expected to provide specific and solid reasons for any conclusions he makes. He therefore tries his best to dig up what evidence he can, although in his heart he has already concluded that Light is Kira, even before the "second Kira" appears. L sets up the investigation and its headquarters simply to find proof to support his supposition. L will no longer allow his mind to be changed, no matter what happens.

On the videotape, the second Kira suggests the two Kira's "show each other our shinigami." L reacts very strongly to the word "shinigami"—he even falls over backwards. The reason is that the first Kira had one of his heart-attack victims write out a message mentioning "shinigami." To L, it is unlikely that the first Kira and the second Kira, who apparently have no contact with each other yet, would both cryptically use the word "shinigami." The second Kira shouldn't even know that Kira used the word. L is forced to acknowledge the existence of shinigami. The viewers know this to be true, but, for most of the characters, this is not plausible at all.

So, L goes down the road of treating "shinigami" as merely a word indicating whatever power or powers the Kiras have. Then, when a "diary" shows up along with a videotape sent by the second Kira and says "At the Giants match at Tokyo Dome, we show each other our shinigami," L and the other investigators take it as a message from the second Kira for the two Kiras to meet at Tokyo Dome on the day of the entry. But what Misa, the second Kira, actually meant to get across to Kira (Light) was the entry, "I meet a friend in Aoyama. We show each other our notebooks." Light catches onto this, since

Kira and the second Kira both use notebooks—Death Notes—to kill. But L is able to guess that there should be messages hidden elsewhere in the diary, to the point that, observing that there are two other locations specified with dates—Aoyama on the 22nd and Shibuya on the 24th—he urges searching those places on those days as well.

50 If L gets so close, why is his attention never fixed on the word "notebook"?

The 22nd: "I meet a friend in Aoyama. We show each other our notebooks." The phrases "meet" and "show each other" are the keys. The videotape also said "show each other"—"show each other our shinigami." When "show each other" appears again here, a genius like L, who normally is alert to the smallest of clues, would be expected to take notice, recognize this part as crucial, and question whether "notebooks" has something to do with "shinigami." For a detective normally as perceptive as L, missing this is a serious and unusual blunder.

When L sees the tape from the second Kira that Light has Misa make, he deduces from the change in the second Kira's attitude that the first and second Kiras must have met. Even Light, who gave the instructions for the video, is taken aback at L's insight.

The second Kira leaves evidence for the investigation team, such as fingerprints on the videotapes. However, the evidence doesn't allow them to immediately find Misa. It's not explained in detail exactly how Misa is discovered. However, when L meets Misa on the university campus, he becomes wary of her instantly—in fact, she's already a suspect in his eyes.

L has determined that Kira and the second Kira have now met, and he notices that Misa recognizes Light. Already considering Light and Kira the same, he immediately guesses that Misa is the second Kira. L surreptitiously steals Misa's cell phone.

L had always counted on being able to show his face to Light without being killed, because Light doesn't know his name and L believes Kira cannot kill him without it. The second Kira, it turns out, can kill with just a face. So far, the second Kira hasn't had an opportunity to see L's face. Now, though, on the campus, Misa, the second Kira, sees L's face.

Of course, she has no way of knowing that he is L. Light, of course, knows who he is. This meeting has to look like a surprise, even to Light. However, as soon as Light leaves, he plans to call Misa and have her kill L. This is why L wastes no time in filching Misa's cell phone. If not, he would surely be killed.

Immediately afterwards, the police arrest Misa as the second-Kira suspect, saving L from immediate danger.

52 Why does L release Light and Misa after he gets them locked up?

From the first day L meets Misa, on the college campus, he is out to get her. He is aware that she might not be the second Kira. However, from certain concrete evidence, like a cat's hair from Misa's room found on a videotape sent by the second Kira, L knows that she must be in some way connected to the second Kira. Light, for his part, asks to be locked up. L is already convinced that Light is Kira and therefore concludes that Light has something up his sleeve. And, of course, he's right.

While Misa and Light are locked up, the killings begin anew. This is Light's trick. In advance, he told Rem to give the Death Note to someone else on the condition that the new owner continues the killings. L knows this is a trap. However, Misa and Light have both given up ownership of their Death Notes and thereby have cast away their Death Note memories. This means that L will fail to make them confess, no matter how much he questions them, because they appear to have no knowledge of Kira.

L is forced to try another tactic. By the 50th day of their confinement, he has to release them, even though he still suspects them. Just before that, though, he has Light's father pretend, in front of Misa, that he's going to kill Light. Misa can kill those whose faces she knows, and she loves Light; so if Light appears about to die, she will try to kill Light's father and show her power.

Light's father carries out L's plan. Yet, neither Light nor Misa does anything that could connect them to Kira. It turns into one more failure for L. As such, to succeed, Light's father would probably have to die.

Light and Misa show no signs of guilt. But still L treats them as the two Kiras. L continues his efforts to find proof, but he is eventually killed by Rem.

53 Why is it necessary for Rem to kill L?

When L catches Higuchi, who has been acting as Kira, L finally finds out that Kira's weapon is the Death Note. However, L is wrong-footed by a false rule planted by Light that states that a Death Note owner will die if he or she goes for 13 days without writing another name. This prevents L from being able to immediately catch Light and Misa, because he saw with his own eyes that Light and Misa went for 50 days in captivity without using a Death Note.

Yet, when the Kira killings resume on the very day that surveillance on Misa is lifted, L begins once again to focus on Misa. Rem feels strongly for Misa. She knows that L will go to any means to catch his suspects and that L still suspects Misa and Light. Light shows no signs whatsoever that he intends to protect Misa. If Rem doesn't get involved, she can expect further trouble from L. She has no choice but to kill him.

Rem is ultimately forced to kill L because of L's merciless methods in hunting down criminals.

Chapter 05

Near's and Mello's Secrets

L is famous as a detective worldwide, but very few people know his identity; thus, when he dies, those who know about him are able to keep it a secret and have Light pretend to be L. That makes Light the new head of the Kira investigation, which makes it extremely unlikely that Kira will ever be caught, since Light is Kira and can just pretend to investigate. Light can also now take advantage of L's connections.

On March 12, 2009, the United States of America sets up an agency without any connection to L to hunt for Kira on its own, the Special Provision for Kira (SPK). Its members are selected from the FBI and CIA. Heading it is the young boy Near. One may well ask how a young boy can command such an agency.

Near, like L, comes from an English orphanage called Wammy's House, founded by Watari (Quillsh Wammy is his real name), an inventor, using the funds from his inventions. It's not just an orphanage, though, but a detective training facility that gathers many of the brightest children from around the world and raises them to be detectives. Watari's authority with the government must have helped L rise to a position where he can tell major national agencies such as the FBI what to do. Rem kills Watari, but Roger takes over his position as head of Wammy's House. As a resident of Wammy's House, Near can take advantage of the connections built up by Watari to gain the trust of the FBI and to tell them what to do.

55 Why does Near always have toys with him?

During the Kira investigation, Near is always playing with toys while he tells adults what to do. Some of the adults seem unsettled by this, since it gives the impression that Near isn't taking the situation seriously. Why doesn't Near ever stop playing with his toys to concentrate on serious matters? Perhaps it has to do with Wammy's House's philosophy for nurturing detectives.

L, an older graduate of Wammy's House, always has sweets around while investigating, such as candy bars and cakes. He stacks up sugar cubes, apparently for fun. Mello, similarly, is always eating chocolate. It may be the case that their detective training at Wammy's House somehow caused them to develop a personality that fixates on certain things. Wammy's House probably encouraged flexible thinking over socially acceptable behavior, and perhaps doing something else while thinking helps its detectives keep their minds open and free. For L and Mello, constantly eating sweets helps them think; for Near, it's playing with toys.

56 Why doesn't Mello take advantage of his origins in Wammy's House?

Mello acts likes a criminal—he uses the Mafia and steals a Death Note—yet his basic motive is the same as Near's, to catch Kira. Why, then, does he not, like Near, take advantage of where he came from and search for Kira from a safer position?

L was Wammy's House's top prodigy, but, when he dies, he needs a successor. Near, in terms of ability, is the most obvious choice. But Mello, a stubborn, competitive person who worshipped L more than anyone else and wanted to be the next L, can't stand to work under Near. He flees Wammy's House and works on his own.

But that's not the only reason. L and Near are "armchair detectives," so to speak, who spend most of their time sitting indoors mentally processing what they know about a case. This isn't Mello's style; his specialty is going out and getting more information. For instance, when he finds out about the Death Note, he wants to get it and study it for himself, regardless of what means that takes. He is gladly willing to go to extremes. To lead an official organization, one can't go to extremes unless one convinces subordinates that such action is justified. Mello would find this constricting. He'd rather be able to do whatever he wants, and this is why he goes off on his own to track down Kira.

S ince Near actually is L's rightful successor, it disturbs him that Light takes on L's name. Another thing that disturbs him is that this new L doesn't seem to be making progress in finding Kira. Yet Light acts pompously, like he is the true successor to L, despite demonstrating little ability. Meanwhile, Kira helps the police get the Death Note back from Mello. Near hears this and begins to wonder if the second L is Kira. Besides the fact that it's strange that the second L, for unclear reasons, trusts the one who claims to be Kira to help in his investigation, what is more strange is that, once they do get the Death Note back from Mello, the other Death Note remains in the possession of the police—Kira gave it to them, and one would expect Kira to take it back.

The police have kept the existence of the Death Note hidden from the public. However, Kira should be horrified that anyone besides him/her possesses a Death Note. Kira is revered as a god because people don't know how he kills. If the public discovered that anyone can kill using the Death Note, the divine awe that surrounds Kira would disappear in a puff of smoke.

The Death Note the police now have is the one that Kira gave to Higuchi to make him the new Kira. When the police catch Higuchi, they acquire the Death Note. This shouldn't be good for Kira. However, not only does Kira work with the police to retrieve the Death Note from Mello, but, even after they succeed, Kira still leaves his Death Note with them. Kira is much too friendly with the police. Maybe he is actually one of them.

Once Near learns all this, he estimates the probability that the second L is Kira as 7 percent, but this is similar to how the first L expressed his suspicion of Light—Near gives a conservative figure but, inside, he's quite sure that the second L is Kira.

58 Why does Near disband the SPK?

After Kira assassinates the U.S. president, the vice-president, on becoming president, announces that the U.S. will no longer investigate the Kira case. In other words, Kira has defeated America. This is when Near disbands the SPK. Since the Special Provision for Kira was founded as a force independent of L, it doesn't have to answer to the rest of the government or coordinate its decisions. Now, since its members are Americans, they may no longer have the freedom they need to find Kira.

However, the real reason Near publicly breaks up the SPK and retains only a very small staff is to make it easier for Mello to approach them. Mello has already killed his mafia followers and no longer has an organization of his own. So, if Near gets rid of his own organization, he believes it will be easier for Mello to make contact with him.

It is a gutsy step to give up an organization formed from specially selected FBI and CIA agents, but this move is somewhat mitigated by the fact that most of its members have already been killed, back when Mello had the Death Note. Even without Near breaking up the organization, Mello is able to connect with one of the remaining members, Halle Lidner, and storm into Near's headquarters. Near has been waiting for Mello. He gives him some information about Kira and hopes that Mello will act upon it. Mello does take action and ultimately saves Near's life.

59 Why does Mello make contact with Mogi and bring him to Near?

When Mello comes to Near's secret base, he tells Near about a false Death Note rule (that those who use the Death Note will die if they don't write another name in it within 13 days) in exchange for a photo of him that Near has.

That's all that is revealed, but it appears that Near also at some point speaks to Mello about his suspicions that the second L is Kira. The second Kira is among the Japanese Kira investigation team, with which Mello made contact when he kidnapped Sayu. Mello has met Mogi. Mello tries calling Mogi on the phone. But he brings him to Near. Mello must recognize that Near is, after all, better than him at deduction.

Near tells Mogi that the Death Note's 13-day rule is a lie, and he tries to get him to confess whether anyone at the Japanese investigation ever suspected the second L of being Kira. Because Light was taken off the suspect list after the 13-day rule was discovered, Mogi is put on the spot. But then Light sends a group led by Demegawa to attack the building. In the two days until they narrowly escape, Mogi doesn't speak a word. But he does start to wonder. His comrade in the central investigation, Aizawa, also starts to listen more to Near's argument that the second L is Kira. Mello's contact with Mogi means Light's police allies also start to doubt Light.

60 Why does Near make a point of telling Light that he's going to Japan?

By telling Mogi that the Death Note's 13-day rule is a lie, Near and Mello succeed in making two of the Japanese investigation members, Mogi and Aizawa, suspicious of Light. However, Light is well aware of this. Knowing that Misa is the weakest link in the chain, he has her surrender her Death Note and lose her memory again. Her Death Note is sent to a Kira worshipper named Teru Mikami to continue the Kira killings without the direct involvement of Light or Misa.

That's when Near lays down his challenge to Light by telling him he's coming to Japan. This is risky for Near, since Light could kill him with a Death Note, but Near deduces from the situation that Light isn't in close contact with the new Kira. Light must now be under constant surveillance by Mogi and Aizawa; he couldn't communicate with the new Kira or they would catch him.

Near also realizes that Light is associating with Kiyomi Takada. That's the only person outside the investigation Light is seeing now. She must be his link to the new Kira. Near knows that the real Kira (Light) can't kill only by knowing the target's face. If Near goes to Japan, Light won't necessarily be able to kill him, even if the two meet, because Light doesn't know Near's real name. If Light intends to have the new Kira kill Near, he'll have to bring him to Near (Near doesn't think Light would have the new Kira see his face indirectly, like through a photograph or a surveillance camera).

Near, at the time he decides to go to Japan, doesn't know yet that the new Kira is Mikami. But he does know that Light doesn't have much room to maneuver without giving the new Kira away. If Light tries to kill Near, he'll have to do so without any obvious communication with his subordinates and without attracting suspicion. Now, when Light's hands are tied, is the time for Near to challenge him. This sort of trap, challenging the opponent to attack and thus causing him to let down his guard, is the same type of strategy that L used.

Near intends to confront Light with irrefutable proof that he is Kira and then arrest him. But how does he expect to obtain such proof?

Near needs to get hold of a Death Note in which Light or Mikami has written someone's name. However, because that person will then die, he needs to have Light or Mikami use a fake Death Note. Even if it is fake, if someone writes in it thinking its real, that person is then guilty.

Near arranges for Light and the rest of the central investigation to meet him at a specific time and place, supposedly because he has something related to the Kira case he wants to show them. Light can't come with Death Note in hand. He's already under suspicion as Kira and has no justification to do so unless he is Kira. Therefore, Mikami will be the one who will use the Death Note to kill Near. Near's specification of a time and place, in fact, allows Light to get Mikami to come.

Near already knows that Mikami has the Death Note, and he is hoping Mikami will try to use it. That's why he tells Light the time and place in advance. As long as Near can substitute a fake Death Note, no one will die, and Mikami will give himself away by writing in it. The only thing left is to actually substitute the fake Death Note.

From Light's point of view, it's obvious that Near is planning a trap when he challenges Light. And when he gives him the date and time they should meet in advance, it's clear that Near is intentionally letting him leak that information to the other Kira so that they both turn up. Light also sees that Near will try to do something to Mikami's Death Note. So Light has Mikami use a fake Death Note in advance.

If Mello didn't happen to kidnap Kiyomi Takada, Near would have ended up getting himself and everyone on his side killed. Near's strategy is too simplistic.

After Mello brings Mogi to Near, he never makes direct contact with Near again. So why does he suddenly kidnap Kiyomi Takada?

Mello is close to Halle Lidner, one of Near's associates, as well as Kiyomi Takada's closest bodyguard. Mello must find out from Halle if Takada has contact with Kira. Mello probably intends to make Takada tell him something about Kira. But there is no way to know exactly what he plans to do when he kidnaps her. He whisks her away on his bike and then rides into the back of truck. He then orders her to strip, probably worried about transmitters. He keeps her in the back and drives away.

But Takada still has a piece of a Death Note, and she writes Mello's name on it and kills him. This is what makes it impossible to know exactly for what purpose Mello kidnapped her. However, just as he takes her away, he says, "If I don't do this...," somehow suggesting that kidnapping her is itself the reason.

Mello's kidnapping makes Mikami take out the real Death Note he has been hiding and write Takada's name on it, revealing its existence and location to Near. Mikami assumes that the real Kira, because of his current situation, will not be able to kill Takada himself, so Mikami uses his initiative. But that lets Near know that the Death Note he had Gevanni modify was a fake. So, if Mello hadn't kidnapped Takada, Mikami never would have had to use the real Death Note and Near wouldn't have known the other was a fake. Effectively, Mello saves Near's life (as well as the lives of all those with Near). It's unknown whether Mello actually figures this out himself. It must have somehow been intuition that makes him kidnap Takada.

Chapter 06

Other Secrets

Originally, Misa's fate was to be stabbed to death by a stalker. However, just before this happens, the shinigami Jealous, who has been watching her from the shinigami world, saves her by writing the stalker's name in his Death Note. It's against the rules for shinigami to use the Death Note for the purpose of lengthening a human's life, and Jealous is turned to dust. His remaining life goes to Misa, changing her fate.

Rem, a shinigami who knows Jealous well, becomes interested in this human for whom Jealous sacrificed his own life. She takes the Death Note Jealous leaves behind and gives it to Misa. This makes Misa its new owner and Rem the shinigami in charge of following her, giving Rem license to stay in the human world with Misa. Giving Misa the Death Note is the only way Rem can closely watch over her, since the shinigami world's rules forbid shinigami to enter the human world without a good reason.

Unlike Light, who picks up his Death Note by chance, Misa is specifically given a Death Note by a shinigami. However, even Rem is surprised by the way she never uses it directly for herself. At the time Misa gets the Death Note, she is just starting her career, and so she could use the Death Note to kill rivals, but she doesn't. When she kills, it's always just to meet Kira. (On the other hand, she kills people that Kira wouldn't, such as a television commentator she kills to prove that her video is indeed sent by someone with Kira powers.)

Misa's parents were murdered in front of her by a burglar. However, even though the culprit was arrested, the court had to release him for lack of evidence. However, soon after he is killed by Kira. From then on, she adores Kira and hopes one day to meet him. When she gets the Death Note herself, she realizes she may be able to use it to find Kira. To do so, she sends a video message to Sakura TV that predicts her killings.

Meeting Kira is her reason for living. She doesn't even seem to care about her career much. Therefore, she has no interest in killing people who have nothing to do with Kira.

She even acquires shinigami eyes simply because she notices that the real Kira doesn't have them and that, if she gets them, she may be able to further help Kira.

64 Misa doesn't seem to be very smart, but is she?

As part of her image as a TV "idol," Misa doesn't act very smart. But the evidence suggests that she is actually quite intelligent. When she first attempts to meet Kira, not only does she use a hidden code word that only Kira will understand to secretly draw him to Aoyama, but she does it in a way that allows her to find out who he is without revealing herself (she watches from the inside of a café, in disguise, and looks for a person whose life span she can't see). Also, in the Yotsuba case, she devises and carries out a successful scheme to extract a confession from Higuchi—she tricks him into telling her that he's Kira while recording it on her cell phone.

She rarely shows signs of thinking when she's with Light, but this may be a rational decision. All she cares about is helping Light. She sees him as a genius who can figure out what to do better than she can. Light looks down on her as stupid, but she's actually not. She's both a clever thinker and an effective doer.

65 Is Misa really in love with Light?

Misa admires Kira before she ever meets Light, imagining him to be a young man, and it is this time that she begins to fall in love with the image of him. Then, when she gets her Death Note, she uses it to meet the real Kira, Light. She falls in love with Light knowing that he's Kira, perhaps both because he's Light and because he's Kira. But when L imprisons her, she gives up her Death Note, loses all her memories related to it, and forgets that Light is Kira. But her feelings towards him do not appear to change. This suggests that, even if Misa originally loved Light because he was Kira, she grew to love Light as Light. She can pester him quite a bit sometimes, such as demanding dates, but it's only because of her overwhelming love for him.

W hen she first gets her Death Note, Misa's career as an "idol" consists of occasional magazine appearances, which do not to seem to have gained her any special fame or popularity. When L first meets Misa at university, he says that he not only knows her, but he is a big fan. However, the fact that Misa is locked up immediately afterwards shows that L must have already started investigating her and would know that she was an idol.

The first time Misa visits Light's home, Light's sister Sayu and mother don't know her. (Light asks them not to tell others about their relationship because Misa is a model, and they say, "Oh, so that's why she's so cute," showing that they didn't know.) Yet, in almost no time, when Misa comes to the To-Oh University campus to find Light, students point her out, saying, "Hey, it's Misa," suggesting that she has already become well-known among male students.

When Light and she actually get together, her popularity starts to soar as she goes from commercial appearances to her first feature film role and soon becomes a true Japanese idol. Light has her retire from the entertainment industry when he is hired by the police and acts as the second L. When, later, as part of a plan by Light to "catch Kira" (he is Kira, but, since he is also L and as such the head of the Kira investigation, he has to come up with a plan to "catch Kira" once in a while), it is announced that Misa will be returning to sing in NHN's New Year's Eve Red-and-White Singing Contest (Kohaku Uta Gassen in real life, a famous annual TV tradition on NHK), (the logic being that, since Kiyomi Takada, Kira's messenger, is an NHN newscaster, there must be a link to Kira somewhere within NHN, and Misa, who is closely connected to the police, can naturally infiltrate NHN and even bring policemen along as "bodyguards,") NHN jumps on it and the newspapers triumphantly announce "MISA'S RETURN." Even after a period of retirement, she is still very popular.

67 Is Misa alive at the end?

Near figures out that Light is Kira, and Ryuk writes Light's name in his Death Note. The Kira case is closed. The last chapter shows scenes one year later showing what has become of the other characters involved in it — except for Misa. This brought on a flurry of fan theories on the Internet and such just after Death Note's serialization ended. "If Misa doesn't appear one year later, doesn't that mean she's dead?" "No, if they didn't show what happened to her, she must be still alive. After all, she got Jealous's remaining life span, and that had to have been a lot longer," etc., etc.

However, the writer later stated in an interview that Misa is dead. Although it's not shown, Misa finds out that Light is dead, loses her will to live, and kills herself.

Misa does apparently get the remaining life span of a shinigami, Jealous, but, since Jealous falls in love with her, a human, he probably isn't the type of shinigami to be very aggressive about taking humans' lives in the first place. Therefore, his remaining life span probably isn't after all very much. On top of that, Misa cuts her life span in half twice by her deals for shinigami eyes with Rem and Ryuk. If one looks at it that way, it's no wonder she's dead.

Also, she takes the lives of two shinigami, Jealous and

Rem, before dying herself. To the shinigami, she must be like a time bomb.

Soichiro, with the title of vice-chief of the police headquarters and an unusually firm desire to uphold the law to the letter, frequently comes into conflict with L, who feels it necessary to bend or break the law at times in order to catch Kira.

Even so, Soichiro agrees to have secret cameras placed throughout his house and keep Misa and Light imprisoned for observation. This is because the logic by which L casts suspicion on Misa and Light is too persuasive for him to dismiss. As a father, he does not want to believe that Light, his own son, could be Kira; however, as a police officer, he has learned how to force objectivity on himself, and he goes on forcing himself to objectively suspect his son. To the end, as a father, he doesn't think Light is Kira, but, as a detective, he may suspect he is.

W hen Mello takes Sayu hostage and exchanges her for the Death Note held by the police, Light gives up the ownership of his own Death Note (Rem's) and has Ryuk take it to the police headquarters, saying he was sent by "Kira." Light expects Matsuda to take ownership, obtain the shinigami eyes, enter Mello's hideout, and write Mello's name in the Death Note, after which Light would kill Matsuda to cover the rule he made up that states that anyone who writes in the Death Note will die in 13 days if they don't write another name.

But Light's expectations are thwarted—Soichiro takes the Death Note and the eyes. Soichiro feels responsible for giving the Death Note to Mello's mafia and Light can't stop him. However, it is extremely unlikely that Soichiro Yagami will be able to bring himself to use the Death Note. He can't write Mello's name in it when it matters, and, after they get the Death Note back, he ends up dying in hospital. Although Death Note owners with shinigami eyes can see the life spans of all humans except for other Death Note owners, why doesn't Soichiro see that Light is Kira?

The reason is that, at that time, Light is not a Death Note owner. Sidoh's Death Note has been Snydar's until Snydar dies and it is afterwards given back to Sidoh, Jealous's Death Note is Misa's, and Rem's Death Note is Soichiro's. Therefore, Soichiro sees Light's life span and breathes his last believing that Light isn't Kira. Light made sure in advance not to own any Death Notes when Matsuda got shinigami eyes so that Matsuda wouldn't see that he was Kira, but it ends up allowing his father to die peacefully. Then, once Soichiro is dead, the ownership of Rem's Death Note reverts immediately to Light.

Higuchi is the Kira who continues the killings while Light has forgotten that he is Kira, using a Death Note given to him by Rem. The fact that Higuchi continues the killings while Light is locked up removes suspicion from Light, and, because Higuchi kills too many people (including government officials) who are in the way of his company, Yotsuba, he gets caught. If Rem had picked someone intelligent who thought like Light, someone like Teru Mikami, such a person might not have been caught so easily. Instead, she chooses someone selfish and greedy under Light's command: "Give this notebook to someone who has some status and a lot of ambition who will use it to try to get ahead." Higuchi is the perfect fit.

Light gives up his Death Note ownership and his memory of being Kira, but he is not giving up on being Kira and building the ideal society. To become Kira again, he needs to retrieve the Death Note he gave to Rem. Before the Death Note, Light had a strong sense of justice, like his father, and dreamed of joining the police. If he weren't Kira, he would try to help the investigation track down Kira. Who should Kira be, then, Light must ask himself? Kira should be someone as far removed from his own ideals as possible, someone who would use the Death Note for his own advancement. That would spur him on so that he would definitely see the case through until he came to Kira's real identity. And, indeed, Light manages to observe that "Lately, many people are dying whose deaths would serve the interests of a corporation called Yotsuba." With this, he closes in on Higuchi.

When Light considers what kind of Kira he would hunt down if he lost his memories of the Death Note, it has to be someone like Higuchi. Light has to catch him, and Light can catch him. If the new Kira were too good at being Kira, it would be a problem. Someone like Higuchi, who needs a "death conference" to decide who to kill, makes a perfect temporary Kira.

71 **Why is Teru Mikami chosen to be the next Kira?**

When Light kills L and takes his place, he thinks that there's no one left to threaten him. But then Near shows up, L's true successor. Near smells a rat. Light decides to get public opinion on his side. He pushes America to officially announce it is no longer interested in Kira. He already has control of the Japanese police and the central Kira investigation, giving him little to fear from the authorities. However, he needs the masses to help him squash individuals like Near. Besides, it is essential to his grand scheme that the masses must be won over to Kira. When he is universally worshiped, he believes, crime will disappear from the world. He therefore turns to mass media to get his message across. His first chosen messenger is Demegawa, the director at Sakura TV.

When Light realizes he has come under suspicion again, he decides to create a new Kira away from the central investigation to mislead his doubters. Misa has already fallen under suspicion and therefore is out of the question. Light looks for someone in the media who is intelligent and worships Kira. He finds Teru Mikami on Sakura TV's pro-Kira program.

Because Light isn't able to do anything too fishy, including giving detailed orders to a Death Note user, he needs someone who can do what he would on their own initiative, someone who understands and believes in Light's philosophy of creating peace in the world by destroying anyone who disturbs it. It is also necessary to find someone loyal so that, even if Kira gives him orders from a distance, he won't turn those orders over to the police, but instead feel pride to have been chosen by Kira and execute his orders faithfully.

Teru Mikami meets all the criteria. He surpasses Light's expectations, going so far as to get rid of Demegawa (the Sakura TV director). He chooses Kiyomi Takada as Kira's new messenger without needing to be told, although, in the end, he disappoints Light when he uses the Death Note, revealing Light to be Kira.

Mikami kills Demegawa after deciding that that is what Kira would want. He then picks out Kiyomi Takada as the new messenger to communicate Kira's thoughts through the media. Light is not too pleased initially, since she was one of his girlfriends in college. He wouldn't have chosen someone who could be linked with him. However, he is under pressure from Near and there are rumblings of suspicion from those around him at the central investigation headquarters.

Mikami doesn't know who Kira is or that he has links with Takada. Light realizes that the situation allows him to make contact with his messenger and tell her what to say and do. Takada is the best choice, after all. He is able to meet her as Kira because she already knows him and the Japanese investigation team knows that she used to be Light's girlfriend, making it perfectly natural for him to approach her about the investigation. Light lets Takada know that he is Kira and uses her not only as his messenger, but as an executioner. This is all thanks to Mikami deciding by himself to make Kiyomi Takada Demegawa's successor. It would probably have been too risky for Light himself to make Takada his messenger.

Glossaly

Characters

A

Aiber

Real name Tierry Morrello
Born July 17, 1969

A distinguished professional con man. Thoroughly versed in languages, psychology, persuasion and every other social skill he needs to win over his victims. Even though he is a criminal, he assists L, out of a debt of gratitude.

Andrew Millar

Mafia member. Has been swiping drugs from the organization, but that gets him made an experimental subject for the efficacy of the Death Note when they trade Sayu for it.

Anthony Rester

Real name Anthony Carter.
Born January 6, 1968

Has the title of "Commander" in the SPK. Right-hand man of Near, who somewhat lacks the ability to actualize ideas. Of all the members of the SPK, including those who die, Rester seems to be trusted the most by Near. He has extensive skills, such as lip-reading, that amply justify his position. However, he does not seem to have Near's powers of observation and insight, although he shares Near's primary fault as, compared to the other members, he seems nervous in executing Near's disturbingly unemotional demands for extreme action. He also takes care of Near as if he were his butler. Is Near just lazy or what?

Arayoshi Hatori

Born March 22, 1971

Member of the Yotsuba death conferences. Marketing Strategy Department Head. Married, a father. Looks younger than most of the conference members. Looks strong and tough, but is actually timid. His hobby is pottery. At one special conference, he tells the other members that he doesn't want to participate anymore. The Yotsuba Kira stamps him out as an example.

D

David Hoope

President of the United States of America. In 2009, approves the establishment of the SPK, with Near at its center, in order to get the Death Note. Mello threatens him to get information about the SPK after Mello steals the Death Note. Later, Light, as L, gets him to send special forces to attack the mafia and retrieve the Death Note, but the mission fails, and Kira manipulates him to kill himself with a handgun to keep his mouth shut.

E

Eiichi Takahashi

Born December 19, 1963

Member of the Yotsuba death conferences. Material Projects Department Head and Yotsuba Home Supervisor. Married, a father. Frequently derided by Higuchi during the meetings as "stupid." Long brown hair, with a mustache; wears earrings. Surfs. Graduated from the Business Department at Keiyo University (based on the real-life prestigious Keio University). Despite his top-tier academic background and high company status, he is shallow. Mido puts forward the theory with Namikawa and Shimura that Takahashi's purpose is to be shallower than Kira, to keep Kira hidden.

Ellickson Guardner

Real name: Ellickson Tomas

Member of the SPK. Looks like Steeve Maison. He dies of a heart attack when a spy sent by Mello leaks his identity.

G

George Psyeruth

Vice-President of the United States of America. Becomes President when Hoope dies. However, he is not cut out to be a leader. He immediately bows to Kira's demands, disbands the SPK, and leaks highly classified SPK information to Kira.

Ginzo Kaneboshi

President of a major consumer credit firm. A contemptible man who abuses his debtors, drives them to suicide, and then collects their life insurance payments. Rem writes his name in her Death Note to help Misa prove to Higuchi that she is the second Kira, and he dies of a heart attack.

Gurren Hangfreeze

Real name: Ralph Bey

Rodd Los' direct assistant and a syndicate old-timer.

H

Halle Lidner

Real name: Halle Bullook

The only female member of the SPK. Former CIA investigator. Someone she knew was a victim in the Yotsuba case, boosting her motivation to become part of the SPK. She does her SPK work faithfully and flawlessly, except perhaps for the fact that she gives information about it to Mello. It is difficult to tell what her motives are. As part of an SPK strategy, she becomes Kiyomi Takada's bodyguard and watches her. Her beauty is such that there are magazine articles about it. She dislikes moths.

Hideki Ide

Born September 69, 1969

A National Police Agency detective. He is willing to put his life on the line to catch Kira, but he doesn't trust L, and so he leaves the investigation. Afterwards, he takes on people he can trust and searches for Kira himself. He springs to action in many scenes such as when he comes to pick up Soichiro Yagami, who has crashed into the Sakura TV station to stop the second Kira's broadcast, guarding him with a large police contingent; when he gathers information from Aizawa when Aizawa leaves L's investigation team during the Yotsuba case; and when he stops the speeding Yotsuba Kira, who has gotten shinigami eyes, with an ambush of tinted-window police cars.

Hideki Lyuga (Ryuga)

A popular idol singer, especially among girls, including Sayu. L uses his name when he goes to To-Oh University to meet Light.

Hirokazu Ukita

Born November 9, 1977

A member of the central Kira investigation in Japan. Temperamental and a bit lacking in caution and foresight, but has the courage to get things done. An extremely heavy smoker. He tries to intercept the Kira tape Misa gives, but the second Kira (Misa) blots him out using her shinigami eyes just as he approaches the TV station.

Hitoshi Demegawa

Born April 4, 1966

Director of Sakura TV's Kira programming. An ambitious, avaricious egotist willing to do practically anything for ratings. Broadcasts the announcement tape the second Kira sends to the TV station. Later, he leads a show dedicated to the worship of Kira, but it is too commercial, and Mikami kills him.

I

Ill Ratt

Real name: Sean Danlibi (English spelling uncertain)

CIA investigator, member of the SPK. Actually a spy sent by Mello's mafia. Leaks the existence of the Death Note and information about the SPK.

Isak Gathane

Real name: Joe Morton

Special Forces Commander in the Middle East, under the direct command of U.S. President Hoope. Ordered by Hoope, following Light's request, to retrieve the Death Note from Mello, he attempts to lead a surprise attack on the mafia hideout, but a shinigami named Sidoh, who is helping Mello in the hope of getting his Death Note back, throws off the special forces' helmets, showing their faces and allowing them to be given fatal heart attacks with the Death Note.

J

Jack Neylon

Real name: Kal Snydar

Born February 23, 1973

Mafia member. Has been arrested four times on suspicion of drug and arms dealing, but was released each time on bail for insufficient evidence. Has been part of Rodd Los's syndicate since 1987. Accidentally gets ownership of the Death Note for a time. Makes the bargain with Sidoh for shinigami eyes under threat from Los.

John Matckenraw

Real name: Larry Conars (English spelling uncertain)

FBI chief, member of the SPK. Meets Soichiro Yagami to ask for the Death Note, but only ends up giving away his name.

Jose

Mafia member. When Soichiro Yagami threatens to write Mello's name in the Death Note, Jose shoots him from behind with a Vz61 submachine gun, wounding him fatally. The Japanese investigators kill him with a New Nanbu M60 handgun they carry hidden.

Jun'ichi Yaibe

Otomo Bank Iidabashi Branch Head. The thirteenth Yotsuba death conference has Kira (Higuchi) have him slip on the stairs of his home, fall and die. He dies

thus on September 10, 2004.

K

Kan'ichi Takimura

Japanese National Police Agency chief. Mello's mafia abduct him and force him to tell them about the Death Note stored at the Japanese central investigation headquarters, but Kira shuts him up, manipulating him to hang himself with his necktie.

Kanzo Mogi

Kira investigation code name: "Kan'ichi Moji"

Born September 13, 1973

A member of the central Kira investigation in Japan. A reliable and dutiful detective. He is surprisingly good at cooking. When he takes over Tota Matsuda's post as manager to watch Misa Amane, he shows great acting skills as he takes on the character of a noisy manager, entirely unlike his own personality. He is the first member of the Japanese Kira investigation to meet Near and his assistants in person and gradually begins to wonder if Light really is Kira.

Kazuhiko Hibima

Principal newscaster on Taiyo (Sun) TV. Against Kira. Because of his frequent on-air condemnation of Kira, the second Kira announces on Sakura TV that he will die of a heart attack during a live news broadcast at 6:00 p.m. on April 18, 2004.

Subsequently, he does.

Ken Yadanaka

A prisoner used by Light to test the extent to which he can manipulate victims' actions before their death. On December 19, 2003, he writes a message claiming he fears Kira and then dies of a heart attack.

Kiichiro Osoreda

Robs a bank, kills three, and escapes. Then, manipulated by Light on December 20, 2003, hijacks a bus. He touches a piece of the Death Note and is able to see Ryuk. Panicking, he shoots wildly at Ryuk with his pistol and then tries to run, but gets hit and killed by a car when he leaves the bus. To others, his behavior is easily explained by his drug addiction; he is assumed to have been hallucinating.

Kiyomi Takada

Born July 12, 1985

The same year as Light in To-Oh University. So beautiful she is called "Miss T.U." Haughty. A Kira supporter. Teru Mikami picks her as the new representative for Kira after he kills Demegawa, a post she thereafter carries out on NEWS9. Light then has her act as his contact with Mikami, whom he can't contact directly, and, when Gevanni shadows Mikami, Light has her do his killing using Death Note paper. She's wrapped around Light's finger. When Mello kidnaps her, she kills him with a

Death Note scrap, in addition to carrying out Light's commands to kill as many criminals as possible. However, Light and Mikami both write for her to be burned to death in order to destroy evidence, and she is discovered as a burned corpse.

Koji Aoi

Aoi Manufacturing's System Integration Department Vice-Head. The third Yotsuba death conference asks Kira to have him die of cancer, but it fails because they specify the time. Instead, on July 2, 2004, he dies of a heart attack.

Koki Tanakabara

Announcer for NHN Golden News. When the police storm Sakura TV upon its broadcast of a tape by the second Kira and seal the area off, Tanakabara asserts that "This is what is right for a lawful nation to do," opposing Kira head-on, even going so far as to explicate his name on air.

Koreyoshi Kitamura

National Police Agency vice-chief. Soichiro Yagami's superior. Gets the impression that his daughter may be under suspicion when FBI agent Raye Penber investigates his family with hidden cameras and microphones. During the second Kira case, under L's direction, sends police to the Sakura TV station to save Soichiro, who has broken in to take the video with the second Kira's message and killing forewarnings from Demegawa.

In the Yotsuba case, under pressure from government officials bribed by Kira, he forbids Soichiro to continue to investigate with L and forces his resignation.

Kuro Otoharada

The first Death Note victim in the story. On November 27, 2003, he murders six in Shinjuku; on November 28, he invades a nursery school and takes eight teachers and children hostage. As Light watches this on television, he tries out the Death Note on him, and Otoharada dies of a heart attack.

Kyosuke Higuchi

Born June 6, 1972

Member of the Yotsuba death conferences. Research and Development Laboratory Head. Single. Greedy for promotion and money. Stands out for his cruel, tactless manner of speaking (his family name means "Firemouth"). Demoted from the position of Research and Development Department Head because of poor performance and personal problems. After Rem gives him a Death Note, along with continuing the Kira killings, he kills anyone who stands, or potentially could stand, in Yotsuba's way. Eventually, though, he's discovered, caught by the police, and killed when light writes his name on a scrap of Death Note paper.

L

L

Also known as Lyuzaki (Ryuzaki), Lyuga (Ryuga), Erald Coil and Danuve

Real name, according to DEATH NOTE 13 HOW TO READ, is L Lawliet

Born December 31, 1979

The world's greatest detective, he has solved a number of complex cases around the world and is known as "the secret top" and "the final trump card." He will go to any means to solve a case, even breaking the law himself to chase down Misa and Light as he struggles to close the Kira case. However, Rem, a shinigami, writes his name in her Death Note and kills him.

Light Yagami

Born February 28, 1986

As a student at Great Nation Academy Private High School, he consistently scores top in Japan on national tests, looks up to his police officer father, Soichiro, and hopes one day to join the police force himself. When he picks up a Death Note Ryuk dropped in the human world because he was bored, his life changes forever as he tries to build what he believes is an ideal society by eliminating criminals with the Death Note, eventually becoming worshiped by the public as "Kira." Meanwhile, however, he hides the fact that he is Kira and enters Japan's top university, To-Oh University (in real life, it's the University of Tokyo).

After he graduates, he joins the police, a dream he has had since childhood, calls himself L and takes over as head of the Kira investigation.

Lind L. Tailor

Claims to be L, the one person whom police anywhere in the world will follow, but is actually a death-row criminal kept hidden by the police from the public. Acting as L, he appears on live television, supposedly broadcast simultaneously around the world, promising the capture of Kira and condemning his actions as evil. This angers Light, who writes Tailor's name in the Death Note, causing him to die of a heart attack. However, this only reveals, not only to L, but also to the general public, that Kira can kill without direct contact, as well as revealing to L, who also considers Kuro Otoharada's death, that Kira is in the Kanto region of Japan, since it was actually only broadcast there.

M

Maigoro Tomi

Works at a café in Shinjuku Station. Arrested several times on charges of sexual assault, but released each time for insufficient evidence. He dies of a heart attack at 3:05 p.m. on December 27, 2003 so that Light can show Raye Penber that he is Kira.

Masahiko Kida

Born October 20, 1971

Member of the Yotsuba death conferences. Light Projects Department Head. Married. Joined Yotsuba in 1994. Calm and calculating, but too inflexible to be able to deal well with unexpected situations. Wears glasses. Collecting spectacles is his hobby. Assigned to contact Erald Coil, whom the death conference hires to find out who L is, and manage the conference's funds.

Masaaki Shirami

Born August 1, 1955

Five-time arsonist who has caused 13 deaths. He is arrested in the midst of another arson attempt on November 15, 2003. While he is in jail, on December 19, 2003, Light uses him for an experiment in manipulating victims' actions before their death, successfully causing him to cut his finger, draw a pentagram on the wall of his cell with the blood, and then die of a heart attack.

Matsujiro Nakaokaji

Born June 6, 1960

A six-time robber-murderer, he has killed with his infamous knife one pachinko hall employee, two convenience store clerks, and two karaoke box staff. Used by Light for an experiment in manipulating victims' actions before death in preparation for his plan to use Kiichiro Osoreda to uncover Raye Penber.

Matt

Real name Mail Jeevas (according to DEATH NOTE 13 HOW TO READ).

Born February 1, 1990

Becomes one of Mello's Kira investigation assistants after Mello's mafia die. He is always wearing goggles and smokes constantly. Boyish looks. Prefers playing games over going out and has little interest in the affairs of the world. Mello trusts him, but the details of their relationship are unknown.

Mello

Real name: Mihael Keehl

Born December 13, 1989

Raised in an orphanage Watari founded to produce L and successors, called Wammy's House and located in Winchester, Hampshire, England. With Near, one of the two selected to be L's successors. Has seen Near as a rival since childhood. In contrast to Near, he is bold and active, with the flip side that he acts on impulse and doesn't look where he's going. He is emotionally tempestuous, prone to deep jealousy, stubborn, and prideful. He loves chocolate bars; he is always munching on one. He is willing to do anything it takes to catch Kira, even if it means committing crimes: for instance, he joins the mafia and threatens the police to get a Death Note, kills his mafia underlings, and kidnaps Kiyomi Takada, Kira's messenger.

Misa Amane

Born December 25, 1984

Starts out as a model for teen magazines. Acquires a Death Note that belonged to shinigami Jealous, who saves her from a stalker. Admires Kira as the one who punished the killer of her parents. When she gets the Death Note, she realizes that Kira uses a Death Note too, and, from Kyoto, sets out to Tokyo to find Kira. She becomes known as the "second Kira" as she succeeds in meeting Kira (Light), but L hunts her down and imprisons her. She gets out of it by abandoning her Death Note, hidden by Light, and her memory of it, but Light gets it back to her later. Her love for Light becomes the sole meaning of her life as Light accepts her as his girlfriend.

N

Naomi Misora

Born February 11, 1976

Raye Penber's fiancée. Former FBI investigator. It is said she became an FBI investigator exceptionally quickly despite being a woman. When she gets engaged to Penber, she retires from the FBI. She goes with Penber to Japan to meet her parents on the same trip, but then Penber is killed by Kira. Through her grief, she investigates the bus-jacking incident in which Penber was involved as well as the death of a convenience store robber eight hours earlier and realizes that Kira can kill by means other than heart attacks and that Kira learned Penber's name on the bus as one of the passengers. Light, however, catches onto her and kills her with the Death Note.

Near

Real name Nate River; also known as N

Born August 24, 1991. Raised in an orphanage Watari founded to produce L and successors, called Wammy's House and located in Winchester, Hampshire, England. With Mello, one of the two selected to be L's successors. Near and Mello then leave Wammy's House, and Near eventually wins an audience with the President of the United States, David Hoope, and is entrusted to lead a new organization formed specially against Kira, the Special Provision for Kira (SPK). (Near somehow has the support of an FBI chief named Mason.) He lets the "second L," Light, know that he is L's true successor, calling himself N. He constantly plays with puzzles, models, cards, dice, finger puppets and other such toys.

R

Raye Penber

Born December 31, 1974

An FBI investigator. Japanese-American. Assigned to investigate the Kitamura and Yagami households on L's request after L surmises that Kira is close to the Japanese police. When shadowing Light Yagami, the bus they are on is hijacked and he ends up showing L his FBI identification card. He is then threatened by Kira, and by doing so, helps bring about the deaths of the other FBI agents in Japan before he dies of a heart attack himself three seconds after getting off the Yamanote Line.

Reiji Namikawa

Born August 3, 1974

Member of the Yotsuba death conferences. Primary Sales Department Head. Single. Conspicuous long, black hair. Extremely intelligent and perceptive. The youngest member of the conferences, but stands out as a leader from his speech. Plays shogi (Japanese chess) at the level of a 4-dan pro. Lived in America for six years. His father is the president of Yotsuba America.

Rodd Los

Real name: Dwhite Godon

Born April 13, 1968

Mafia don with skinhead. Cold and cruel. Like Mello, he will use any means to his ends. Has absolute faith in Mello, who burst brazenly into his scene a year and a half previous.

Roger Ruvie

Born April 29, 1939

In charge of Wammy's House, the orphanage established by Quillsh Wammy (Watari) to create L and successors. Very close to Wammy. Near's effective guardian.

Roppei Tamiya

Akamaru Shoji Development Projects Department Head. The second Yotsuba death conference decides that Kira (Higuchi) should make him die by crashing through the wall as he speeds along the bay, as he is wont to do. However, it happens to be impossible for him to be at the bay, so it doesn't work. Instead, on June 27, 2004, he dies of a heart attack in Italy.

Roy

Mafia member. He is one of the last of the mafia to survive with Mello when Kira massacres them. When he and Mello try to run away with the Death Note, however, the Japanese central investigation stops him.

Rushuall Bid

Real name: Al Meam

Like Gurren Hangfreeze, he is Rodd Los' talented close assistant.

S

Sachiko Yagami

Maiden name: Tanaka

Born October 10, 1962

Light's mother. A housewife. Proud of Light's success as a student. Never learns that Light is Kira.

Sayu Yagami

Born June 18, 1989

Light's little sister. Cheerful and energetic, and, unlike Light, ingenuous. Often asks Light for help with school work. Loves Light and her father. A major fan of the popular singer Hideki Ryuga. The trauma she suffers when Mello takes her hostage to get the Death Note from the police puts her in hospital.

Shingo Mido

Born January 25, 1972

Member of the Yotsuba death conferences. Management Strategy Department Head and Yotsuba Finance Supervisor. Single. Calm and contemplative, his analytical skills are excellent. Since his father is in the House of Councilors, he uses his political connections to help Yotsuba Kira (Higuchi).

Shuichi Aizawa

Kira investigation code name: "Aihara"

Born May 11, 1969

A member of the central Kira investigation in Japan. When Soichiro Yagami temporarily resigns from the police, he becomes the new head of the police investigation headquarters. He finds L's methods questionable and untrustworthy. When the police administration in charge of the Kira investigation decides to close it down, under pressure from government officials, Aizawa, uncomfortable with losing his job, decides to leave the Kira investigation. He finds out that L has prepared in advance funds to support each of the investigators comfortably for the rest of their lives and was just testing who would resign, but that only makes Aizawa more angry. Even after he separates from L's group, he retains his strong sense of justice and his commitment to the capture of Kira, and he goes after Kira on his own. After the capture of Higuchi, he and the others reunite.

Skeer (English spelling uncertain)

Mafia member. He is one of the last of the mafia to survive with Mello when Kira massacres them. Fights the Japanese central investigation to protect the Death Note, but fails.

Soichiro Yagami

Kira investigation code name: "Shijuro Asahi"

Born July 12, 1955

Light Yagami's father. Head of the National Police Agency bureau of investigation, as well as of the Kira investigation. An upright, kind-hearted man who dearly loves his family and passionately devotes himself to his job, he earns intimate trust from his subordinates. However, because of his high respect for the law and regard for human life, he has doubts about L's investigation methods. After his daughter Sayu is kidnapped and he gives Mello a Death Note to get her back, he feels a deep-seated sense of responsibility and volunteers to be the one to shorten his own life to get the shinigami eyes that may be important for

getting the Death Note back. He breathes his last in hospital with the Kira case still in progress.

Steeve Maison

FBI chief, member of the SPK. Early on, he is the one who, at L's request, sends the 12 FBI agents to Japan to search for traces of Kira among those connected to the Japanese police. When the agents are killed and their mission comes to light, Maison, fearing that Kira will judge him responsible, cuts his support for L.

Stephen Gevanni

Real name: Stephen Loud

Member of the SPK. Black hair, young-looking. While the SPK is in America, he is in charge of its communication systems, radar, and other electronic operations. In Japan, he is entrusted with eavesdropping and following Mikami (X-Kira). He is able to make a replica of Mikami's Death Note in one night.

Suguru Shimura

Born July 21, 1968

Member of the Yotsuba death conferences. Human Resources Department Personnel Section Head. Single. More than anyone else in the conference, he seems weak and nervous, but he really has the ability to see the important signs and get to root of the matter. He can even read Namigawa's poker face. In high school, he was selected to represent Japan in rugby.

T

Takeshi Ooi

Born March 31, 1961

Member of the Yotsuba death conferences. VT Operations Department Head. Single. The hefty bald-headed man who consistently opens the meetings. Always wears sunglasses. Clear-headed and decisive, but a bit rough. His father works for the Japanese Department of Defense (based on the real-life Ministry of Defense).

Takeyoshi Moriya

Former Yotsuba Group Chairman. The seventh Yotsuba death conference asks Kira to have him die of disease, but, as in the case of Koji Aoi, it fails because they specify the time. Instead, on July 30, 2004, he dies of a heart attack.

Takuo Shibuimaru

The second victim of the Death Note. Light experiments on him on his way home from cram school.

Tazakichi Yoda

A prisoner used by Light to test the extent to which he can manipulate victims' actions before their death. On December 19, 2003, he runs out of his cell and into the employee restroom, dying at 6 p.m. of a heart attack.

Teru Mikami

Near refers to him as "X-Kira"

Born June 7, 1982

A detective. Adores, trusts and worships Kira, referring to him as a "god," in a manner quite unsettling. Light, knowing this, has him take ownership of Misa's Death Note. For Kira's sake, he makes the bargain for the shinigami eyes, and, as Kira's agent, he judges the world's criminals. When Mello kidnaps Takada, however, he mistakenly assumes that the real Kira isn't in a position to be able to kill Takada, and so he takes out the real Death Note he has been hiding in a safe to do the killing himself, revealing to Near the fact that he had been using a fake note to trick Near. Then, when Near's assistant Gevanni substitutes a fake Death Note for the real one and Mikami tries to use it, he gives away the fact that Light is Kira because he writes the names of all the Kira investigators except Light.

Tokio Yakoda

Otomo Bank Supervisor. The 15th Yotsuba death conference has Kira (Higuchi) have him commit suicide after hearing from the police that he is suspected of bribery. He dies thus on October 1, 2004.

Tota Matsuda

Kira investigation code name: "Taro Matsui"

Born December 14, 1978

A member of the central Kira investigation in Japan. Goofy and rather dense, he is not very good at being a detective; he mentions casually at one point that he only got into the police because of a connection. However, he has a strong sense of right and wrong. On the other hand, he sometimes sounds sympathetic to Kira. When he is assigned to keep an eye on Misa Amane as he acts as her manager, he seems right at home, leading many fans to suggest he really should be in the entertainment industry. He tends to act on impulse without considering the consequences, and he trusts Light more than L. But he shows exceptional prowess with a gun (even in the live-action movie version).

W

Watari

Real name: Quillsh Wammy
Born May 1, 1933

An elderly gentleman who serves as L's right-hand man and his contact and representative with governments, organizations and individuals worldwide. Quillsh Wammy is a celebrated inventor. Uses the funds from his inventions to establish orphanages around the world. One of them, Wammy's House, run by a man called Roger, raises gifted children to be detectives. Rem kills him with her Death Note along with L.

Wedy

Real name Merrie Kenwood

A distinguished professional thief. She can break through and pass any kind of lock, safe or security device. Even though she is a criminal, she is close to L, who has her break into and search Yotsuba. Unlike Aiber, she is willing to carry and use a gun. An American citizen.

Y

Y462 (name unknown)

Mafia member. Meets Soichiro Yagami to exchange Sayu for the Death Note. Testing the Death Note first, he succeeds, but Los says he still needs to pay for his mistakes in the past and blows up his helicopter.

Yamamoto

Only appears in the final chapter. A new member of the Japanese Central Investigation Headquarters. Friends with Matsuda, with whom he often drinks.

Z

Zakk Irius

Mafia member. When Light's sister Sayu is kidnapped, Zakk Irius leads Light's father Soichiro to the place where he can give the mafia the Death Note in exchange.

Shinigami

Ryuk

Male

Shinigami rank 6

Originally allows Light to get hold of a Death Note. It originally belongs to Sidoh, who accidentally dropped it in the shinigami world. Ryuk gets hold of it by pretending to the shinigami king that it was he who dropped it. Because he is bored, he writes "DEATH NOTE" on the cover and rules inside, drops it in the human world, and waits for someone to use it. Light becomes its first human owner, and Ryuk haunts him, telling him that he's going to enjoy watching what Light will do without getting involved. However, he does occasionally help Light for apples, which he loves. At the end, watching Light demand his help against Near, Ryuk decides that nothing more interesting is going to come of it, says to Light, "It's been nice passing all this time with you," and writes Light's name in his fatal Death Note.

Rem

Female

Shinigami rank 4

The shinigami who gives Misa her Death Note (originally Jealous's). Meets Jealous at the hole in the shinigami world for looking at the human world and watches Misa with him. After he dies, she goes down to the human world and gives Misa his Death Note. Seems more serious than most of the shinigami, with detailed knowledge of the rules of the Death Note. Her shinigami rank is high. She has a strong motherly affection for Misa; everything she does is for her sake, and she will do anything she can that Misa asks. This sometimes causes her to help Light out.

When, by Light's plan, Misa gets stuck between a rock and hard place, Rem saves her from getting caught by writing the names of L and Watari in her own Death Note, thereby turning to ash (because she used her Death Note to save a human).

Jealous

Male

Shinigami rank 13

The original owner of the Death Note Rem gives Misa. Has the lowest rank of all the shinigami who appear. Uncharacteristically for a shinigami, his personality is kind and gentle, and he falls in love with a human, Misa. Killing the stalker who was supposed to kill Misa, he dies: "If the god of death decides to use the DEATH NOTE to kill the assassin of an individual he favors, the individual's life will be extended, but the god of death will die."

Sidoh

Male

Shinigami rank 8

The original owner before Ryuk of the Death Note Light picks up. He looks very scary, but he's a bit stupid and somehow lovable. He goofs off from taking lives until his life span is almost at an end and doesn't notice until then that he's been missing his Death Note for six years. He goes to tell the King of Death, but it turns out that Ryuk has already tricked the king out of Sidoh's Death Note, and so Sidoh goes down to the human world to try to get it back. When Light finally gives it back to him, he happily returns home.

His name is spelled "Shidoh" in DEATH NOTE 13 HOW TO READ, but "Sidoh" in the character introduction pages in the manga proper, as well as in the English translation.

King of Death

At the top of all the shinigami, and in charge of the Death Notes. Very little is known about him. He keeps Sidoh's Death Note as lost property, but he is tricked out of it by Ryuk. However, since he seems to pay little attention when Sidoh tells him, he can't care that much about such things. Almost all the shinigami refer to him as "Gramps." He is only mentioned and never appears.

Armonia Jastin Beyondllemason

Male

Shinigami rank 2

He has the fullest grasp of the laws of the shinigami world and the rules of the Death Note. He resembles a golden skeleton covered in jewels, even having gems for eyes. Not only is he extremely knowledgeable about the rules, but, unlike other shinigami, he is quite willing to answer the questions of the other shinigami. He must do it a lot.

Dalil Guillohrtha

Female

Shinigami rank 3

Wreathed in metal. Has no interest in the human world and spends her time stacking skulls. Despite being female, she uses a male pronoun for herself ("ore").

Dellidublly

Male

Shinigami rank 10

A gambler. With a huge sickle, his appearance is how most people imagine shinigami (a concept that originated in the West).

Gook

Male

Shinigami rank 7

A friend of Ryuk's. Frequently gambles with Dellidublly, but has never once won.

Zerhogie

Male

Shinigami rank 5

The oldest-looking shinigami. He appears with a hook on his left hand and a large feather decoration around his body. Begins to take an interest in the human world after he hears that Ryuk is staying there.

Calikarcha

Male

Shinigami rank 11

Looks like an alien. Has multiple eyes in a line on one side of his head.

Kinddara Guivelostain

Female

Shinigami rank 12

Wild and violent, and has no desire to do anything but make mayhem. Doesn't appear in the manga.

Nu

Female

Shinigami rank 1

Looks like a big rock with tens of eyes all over her body. The second-most powerful shinigami after the King. Does not appear in the manga.

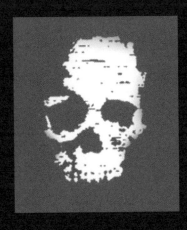

DEATH NOTE - HOW TO USE IT

I

The human whose name is written in this note shall die.

This note will not take effect unless the writer has the person's face in their mind when writing his/her name. Therefore, people sharing the same name will not be affected.

If the cause of death is written within 40 seconds of writing the person's name, it will happen.

If the cause of death is not specified, the person will simply die of a heart attack.

After writing the cause of death, details of the death should be written in the next 6 minutes and 40 seconds.

II

This note shall become the property of the human world, once it touches the ground of (arrives in) the human world.

The owner of the note can recognize the image and voice of its original owner, i.e. a god of death.

The human who uses this note can neither go to Heaven nor Hell.

III

If the time of death is written within 40 seconds after writing the cause of death as a heart attack, the time of death can be manipulated, and the time can go into effect within 40 seconds after writing the name.

The human who touches the DEATH NOTE can recognize the image and voice of its original owner, a god of death, even if the human is not the owner of the note.

IV

The person in possession of the DEATH NOTE is possessed by a god of death, its original owner, until they die.

If a human uses the note, a god of death usually appears in front of him/her within 39 days after he/she uses the note.

Gods of death, the original owners of the DEATH NOTE, do not do, in principle, anything which will help or prevent the deaths in the note.

A god of death has no obligation to completely explain how to use the note or rules which will apply to the human who owns it.

V

A god of death can extend his life by putting human names on the note, but humans cannot.

A person can shorten his or her own life by using the note.

The human who becomes the owner of the DEATH NOTE can, in exchange of half of his/her remaining life, get the eyeballs of the god of death which will enable him/her to see a human's name and remaining lifetime when looking through them.

A god of death cannot be killed even if stabbed in his heart with a knife or shot in the head with a gun. However, there are ways to kill a god of death, which are not generally known to the gods of death.

VI

The conditions for death will not be realized unless it is physically possible for that human or it is reasonably assumed to be carried out by that human.
The specific scope of the condition for death is not known to the gods of death, either. So, you must examine and find out.

VII

One page taken from the DEATH NOTE, or even a fragment of the page, contains the full effects of the note.
The instrument to write with can be anything, ((e.g. cosmetics, blood, etc)) as long as it can write directly onto the note and remains as legible letters.
Even the original owners of the DEATH NOTE, gods of death, do not know much about the note.

VIII

You may also write the cause and/or details of death prior to filling in the name of the individual. Be sure to insert the name in front of the written cause of death. You have about 19 days (according to the human calendar) in order to fill in a name.
Even if you do not actually possess the DEATH NOTE, the effect will be the same if you can recognize the person and his/her name to place in the blank.

IX

The DEATH NOTE will not affect those under 780 days old.
The DEATH NOTE will be rendered useless if the victim's name is misspelled four times.

X

"Suicide" is a valid cause of death. Basically all humans are thought to possess the possibility to commit suicide. It is, therefore, not something "unbelievable to think of".

Whether the cause of the individual's death is either a suicide or accident, If the death leads to the death of more than the intended, the person will simply die of a heart attack. This is to ensure that other lives are not influenced.

XI

Even after the individual's name, the time of death, and death condition on the DEATH NOTE were filled out, the time and condition of death can be altered as many times as you want, as long as it is changed within 6 minutes and 40 seconds from the time it was filled in. But, of course, this is only possible before the victim dies.

Whenever you want to change anything written on after you wrote, you must first rule out the characters you want to erase with two straight lines.

As you see above, the time and condition of death can be changed, but once the victim's name has been written, the individual's death can never be avoided.

XII

If you lose the DEATH NOTE or have it stolen, you will lose its ownership unless you retrieve it within 490 days.

If you have traded the eye power of a god of death, you will lose the eye power as well as the memory of the DEATH NOTE, once you lose its ownership. At the same time, the remaining half of your life will not be restored.

XIII

You may lend the DEATH NOTE to another person while maintaining its ownership. Subletting it to yet another person is possible, too.

The borrower of the DEATH NOTE will not be followed by a god of death. The god of death always remains with the owner of the DEATH NOTE. Also, the borrower cannot trade the eyesight of the death.

XIV

When the owner of the DEATH NOTE dies while the Note is being lent, its ownership will be transferred to the person who is holding it at that time.

If the DEATH NOTE is stolen and the owner is killed by the thief, its ownership will automatically be transferred to the thief.

XV

When the same name is written on more than two DEATH NOTES, the Note which was first filled in will take effect, regardless of the time of death,.
If writing the same name on more than two DEATH NOTES is completed within a 0.06-second difference, it is regarded as simultaneous; the DEATH NOTE will not take effect and the individual written will not die.

XVI

The god of death must at least own one DEATH NOTE. That DEATH NOTE must never be lent to or written on by a human.
Exchanging and writing on the DEATH NOTE between the gods of death is no problem.

XVII

If the god of death decides to use the DEATH NOTE to kill the assassin of an individual he favors, the individual's life will be extended, but the god of death will die.
The dead god of death will disappear, but the DEATH NOTE will remain. The ownership of this DEATH NOTE is usually carried over to the next god of death that touches it, but it is common sense that it is returned to the Great god of death.

XVIII

Only by the touching each other's DEATH NOTE can human individuals who own the DEATH NOTE in the human world recognize the appearance or voice of each other's god of death.

An individual with the eye power of god of death can tell the name and life span of other humans by looking at that persons face. By possessing the DEATH NOTE, an individual gains the ability to kill and stops being a victim. From this point, a person with the DEATH NOTE cannot see the life span of other DEATH NOTE owners, including him/herself. But, it is not really necessary for the individual to view the life span of him/herself nor other DEATH NOTE owners.

The god of death must not tell humans the names or life spans of individuals he sees. This is to avoid confusion in the human world.

XVIV

It is prerequisite for the DEATH NOTE used in the human world that a living god of death makes sure that the humans in the human world use it.

It is very difficult to consider that a god of death who has possessed a human could die, but if he should die, the DEATH NOTE that he brought into the human world will not lose its power.

XX

In order to see the names and life spans of humans by using the eye power of the god of death, the owner must look at more then half of that person's face. When looking from top of bottom, he must look at least from the head to the nose. If he looks at only the eyes and under, he will not be able to see the person's name and life span. Also, even though some parts of the face, for example the eyes, nose or mouth are hidden, if he can basically see the whole face, he will be able to see the person's name and life span. It is still not clear how much exposure is needed to tell the name and life span, and this needs to be verified.

If above conditions are met, names and life spans can be seen through photos and pictures, no matter how old they are. But this is sometimes influenced by the vividness and size. Also, names and life spans cannot be seen by face drawings, however realistic they may be.

XXI

Those with the eye power of the god of death will have the eyesight of over 3.6 in the human measurement, regardless of their original eyesight.

XXII

The individuals who lose the ownership of the DEATH NOTE will also lose their memory of the usage of the DEATH NOTE. This does not mean that he will lose all the memory from the day he owned it to the day he loses possession, but means he will only lose the memory involving the DEATH NOTE.

XXIII

Whenever an individual with ownership of more than two DEATH NOTES loses possession to one of the DEATH NOTES, he will not be able to recognize that DEATH NOTES god of death's appearance or voice anymore. The god of death himself will leave, but all the memory involving that DEATH NOTE will remain as long as he maintains ownership of at least one other DEATH NOTE.

XXIV

The god of death must not stay in the human world without a particular reason. Conditions to stay in the human world are as follows:
I. When the god of death's DEATH NOTE is handed to a human.
II. Essentially, finding a human to pass on the DEATH NOTE should be done from the world of the gods of death, but if it is within 82 hours this may also be done in the human world.
III. When a god of death stalks an individual with an intention to kill them, as long as it is within 82 hours of haunting them, the god of death may stay in the human world.

XXV

The god of death must not hand the DEATH NOTE directly to a child under 6 years of age (based on the human calendar).
The DEATH NOTE must not be handed to a child under 6 years of age, but DEATH NOTES that have been dropped into the human world, and are part of the human world, can be used upon humans of any age with the same effect.

XXVI

If you just write, "die of accident" for the cause of death, the victim will die from a natural accident after 6 minutes and 40 seconds from the time of writing it.

Even thought only one name is written in the DEATH NOTE, if it influences and cause other humans that are not written in it to die, the victim's cause of death will be a heart attack.

XXVII

If you write, "die of disease" with a specific disease's name and the person's time of death, there must be a sufficient amount of time for the disease to progress. If the set time is too tight, the victim will die of a heart attack after 6minutes and 40 seconds after completing the DEATH NOTE.

If you write, "die of disease" for the cause of death, but only write a specific time of death without the actual name of disease, the human will die from an adequate disease. But the DEATH NOTE can only operate within 23 days (in the human calendar). This is called the 23-day rule.

XXVIII

If you write, "die of disease" like before with a specific disease's name, but without a specific time, if it takes more than 24 days for the human to die the 23-day rule will not take effect and the human will die at an adequate time depending the disease.

When rewriting the cause and/or details of death it must be done within 6minutes and 40 seconds. You cannot change the victim's time of death, however soon it may be.

XXIX

You cannot kill humans at the age of 124 and over with the DEATH NOTE. You cannot kill humans with less than 12 minutes of life left (in human calculations).

XXX

If you have traded the eye power of a god of death, you will see a person's primary life span in the human world.
The names you see with the eye power of a god of death are the names needed to kill that person. You will be able to see the names even if that person isn't registered in the family registration.

XXXI

The number of pages of the DEATH NOTE will never run out.

XXXII

If someone possesses more than one DEATH NOTE, by visualizing the victim, then writing down the name in one of the DEATH NOTES and the cause of death in the other, it will take effect. The order however, is unimportant, if you write down the cause of death in one DEATH NOTE and afterwards, write the name in the other, it will still take effect.
This can also be accomplished by two DEATH NOTE owners working together. In this case, it's necessary that the two touch each other's DEATH NOTES.

XXXIII

If a person loses possession of a DEATH NOTE, they will not recognize the gods of death by sight or voice any more. If however, the owner lets someone else touch his DEATH NOTE, from that time on, that person will recognize the god of death.

In accordance with the above, the human who touched the DEATH NOTE and began to recognize the gods of death's sight and voice, will continue to recognize it until that human actually owns the DEATH NOTE and subsequently looses possession of it.

XXXIV

The owner of the DEATH NOTE cannot be killed by a god of death who is living in the world of the gods of death.

Also a god of death who comes to the human world, in the objective to kill the owner of the DEATH NOTE, will not be able to do so.

Only a god of death that has passed on their DEATH NOTE to a human is able to kill the owner of the DEATH NOTE.

XXXV

If a DEATH NOTE owner accidentally misspells a name four times, that person will be free from being killed by the DEATH NOTE. However, if they intentionally misspell the name four times, the DEATH NOTE owner will die. The person whose name was misspelled four times on purpose will not be free of death by a DEATH NOTE.

XXXVI

There are male and female gods of death, but it is neither permitted, nor possible for them to have sexual relations with humans. The gods of death also cannot have sex with each other.

XXXVII

When regaining ownership of the DEATH NOTE, the memories associated with the DEATH NOTE will also return. In cases where you were involved with other DEATH NOTE as well, memories of all the DEATH NOTES involved will return.
Even without obtaining ownership, memories will return just by touching the DEATH NOTE.

XXXVIII

You will lose memory of the DEATH NOTE when losing its ownership. But you can regain this memory by either obtaining the ownership once again or by touching the DEATH NOTE. This can be done up to 6 times per DEATH NOTE.
If the 6 times are exceeded, the person's memory of the DEATH NOTE will not return and they will have to use it with out any previous memory of it.

XXXIX

Humans that have traded for the eye power of a god of death cannot see the name or life-span of humans who have already passed away by looking their photos.

XL

Whenever a god of death who had been in the human world dies and the DEATH NOTE is left behind and is picked up by a human, that person becomes the owner.

However, in this case, only the human that can recognize the god of death and its voice is able to see and touch the DEATH NOTE.

It is very unlikely, but it by any chance a god of death picks up the DEATH NOTE, that god of death becomes the owner.

XLI

It is useless trying to erase names written in the DEATH NOTE with erasers or white-out.

XLII

The use of the DEATH NOTE in the human world sometimes affects other human's lives or shortens their original life-span, even though their names are not actually written in the DEATH NOTE itself. In these cases, no matter the cause, the god of death sees only the original life-span and not the shortened life-span.

XLIII

If a DEATH NOTE is owned in the human world against the god of death's will, that god of death is permitted to stay in the human world in order to retrieve it.

In that case, if there are other DEATH NOTES in the human world, the gods of death are not allowed to reveal to humans that DEATH NOTE'S owner or its location.

XLIV

If the DEATH NOTE that the god of death owns is taken away; by being cheated by other gods of death and so forth, it can only be retrieved from the god of death who is possessing it at the time. If there is no god of death, but a human possessing it, the only way that the god of death can retrieve it will be to first touch the DEATH NOTE and become the god of death that haunts that human. Then wait until that human dies to take it away before any other human touches it or whenever the human shows a will to let go of it.

XLV

As long as the god of death has at least once seen a human and knows his/her name and life-span, the god of death is capable of finding that human from a hole in the world of the gods of death.

XLVI

There are laws in the world of gods of death. If a god of death should break the law, there are 9 levels of severity starting at Level 8 and going up to Level 1 plus the Extreme Level. For severity levels above 3 the god of death will be killed after being punished.

For example, killing a human without using the DEATH NOTE is considered as the Extreme Level.

XLVII

Losing memory of the DEATH NOTE by passing on the ownership to another, or by abandoning its ownership will only occur when someone is actually killed using that DEATH NOTE. You will not lose memory of the DEATH NOTE, for example, if you merely owned it and had not written anyone's name. In this case, you will not be able to hear the voice or see the figure of the god of death anymore. You will also lose the eye power of the god of death you traded with.

XLVIII

The god of death will not die from lack of sleep. Moreover, gods of death do not really need sleep. The meaning of sleep for gods of death is essentially different from humans and is merely laziness.
Especially gods of death living in the human world that have passed on their DEATH NOTE shouldn't be lazy, as they are required to see the death of the human, but it is not that they are not allowed to sleep.

XLIX

Only 6 DEATH NOTES are allowed to exist at a time in the human world. Of course, the DEATH NOTE that the god of death owns does not count. This means only 6 gods of death that have passed on their DEATH NOTE to humans can stay in the human world.

L

One god of death is allowed to pass on DEATH NOTES to only 3 humans at a time.

It is possible for a single god of death to hand out up to 6 DEATH NOTES, for example, by handing 3 humans 2 DEATH NOTES each.

In other words, one human could own all 6 DEATH NOTE.

LI

However, if a seventh DEATH NOTE is owned by a human in the human world, nothing will happen even if used.

LII

In the event that there are more than 6 DEATH NOTES in the human world, only the first 6 DEATH NOTES that have been delivered to humans will have effect.

The seventh DEATH NOTE will not become active until one of the other 6 DEATH NOTES is burned up, or a god of death takes one of them back to the world of gods of death.

LIII

The DEATH NOTE will not take effect if you write a specific victim's name using several different pages.
But the front and back of a page is considered as one page. For example, the DEATH NOTE will still take effect even if you write the victim's surname on the front page and given name on the back.

LIV

In order to make the DEATH NOTE take effect, the victim's name must be written on the same page, but the cause of death and the situation around the death can be described in other pages of the DEATH NOTE. This will work as long as the person that writes the DEATH NOTE keeps the specific victim's name in mind when writing the cause and situation of the death.

LV

In occasions where the cause and situation of death of death is written as long as they are written within 40 seconds and the causes and situations of the death are not impossible to occur.
In the occasion where the cause of death is possible but the situation is not, only the cause of death will take effect for that victim. If both the cause and the situation ate impossible, that victim will die of heart attack.

LVI

When you write multiple names in the DEATH NOTE and then write down even one cause of death within 40 seconds from writing the first victim's name, the cause will take effect for all the written names.

Also, after writing the cause of death, even if the situation of death is written within 6 minutes and 40 seconds in the human world, that situation will only occur to the victims whom it is possible. For those where the situation is not possible, only the cause of death will occur.

LVII

In the DEATH NOTE you cannot set the death date longer than the victim's original life span. Even if the victim's death is set in the DEATH NOTE beyond his/her original life span, the victim will die before the set time.

LVIII

By manipulating the death of a human that has influence over another human's life, that human's original life span can sometimes be lengthened

If a god of death intentionally does the above manipulation to effectively lengthen a human's life span, the god of death will die, but even if a human does the same, the human will not die.

LIX

A human death caused by the DEATH NOTE will indirectly lengthen some other human's original length of life even without a specific intention to lengthen a particular person's original life span in the human world.

LX

After a god of death had brought the DEATH NOTE to the human world and given its ownership to a human, the god of death may have the right to kill the human using his/her own DEATH NOTE for reasons such as disliking the owner.

LXI

Even if a new victim's name, cause of death, or situation of death is written on top of the originally written name, cause of death or situation of death, there will be no effect on the original victim's death. The same thing will also apply to erasing what was written with a pencil, or whitening out what was written with a pen, in an attempt to rewrite it.

LXII

Once the victim's name, cause of death and situation of death have been written down in the DEATH NOTE, this death will still take place even if that DEATH NOTE or the part of the Note in which it has been written is destroyed, for example, burned into ashes, before the stated time of death.
If the victim's name has been written and then the DEATH NOTE is destroyed in the middle of writing the cause of death, the victim will be killed by heart attack in 40 seconds after writing the name.
If the victim's name and cause of death have been written and the DEATH NOTE is destroyed, like burned, in the middle of writing the situation of death, then the victim will be killed within 6 minutes and 40 seconds via the stated cause of death if the cause is possible within that period of time, but otherwise, the victim will die by heart attack.

LXIII

No matter what medical or scientific method may be employed, it is impossible for humans to distinguish whether or not the human has the eye power of a god of death. Even gods of death cannot distinguish this fact, except for the very god if death that traded his/her eye power with that human.

LXIV

The following situations are the cases where a god of death that has brought the DEATH NOTE into the human world is allowed to return to the world of gods of death.

1. When the god of death has seen the end of the first owner of the DEATH NOTE brought into the human world, and has written that human's name on his/her own DEATH NOTE.

2. When the DEATH NOTE which has been brought in is destroyed, like burned, and cannot be used by humans anymore.

3. If nobody claims the ownership of the DEATH NOTE and it is unnecessary to haunt anyone.

4. If, for any reason, the god of death possessing the DEATH NOTE has been replaced by another god of death.

5. When the god of death loses track of the DEATH NOTE which he/she possesses, cannot identify which human is owning the DEATH NOTE, or cannot locate where the owner is, and therefore needs to find such information through the hole in the world of gods of death.

Even in the situations 2,3, and 4 above, gods of death are obliged to confirm the death of the first owner and write down that human's name in his/her DEATH NOTE even when he/she is in the world of gods of death.

LXV

In the world of gods of death there are a few copies of what humans may call user guidebook for using the DEATH NOTE in the human world. However, the guidebook is not allowed to be delivered to humans.

It is perfectly okay for gods of death to read the guidebook for him/herself and teach humans about its contents, no matter what the content may be.

LXVI

Some limited number of DEATH NOTES have white or red front covers, but they would make no difference in their effects, as compared with the black cover DEATH NOTES.